Letts

KS2 Success SATs

English

D1354365

S

LM 1527777 1

Contents

Speaking and listening

Reading

Writing

Writing

Notes

Answers

Reading aloud

What makes good reading?

Good readers put their nerves to one side and think about what it is like to be a listener. If your listeners cannot understand you, or don't want to listen to you, there is no point reading at all!

Take deep breaths to help you to stay calm and concentrate on reading at a natural pace. When you are nervous, it is very easy to speed up and make mistakes. If you read too slowly, you will sound bored!

Try to forget about your audience. Imagine you are reading to a younger brother or sister instead.

SATs practice

Which of these reading styles would you rather listen to?
Tick the correct box.

LEVEL 3

- Read very quickly, to get it over with. ☐
- Read very slowly, so that the listeners don't miss a word. ☐
- Read at a natural pace, letting punctuation help the reader to decide when to pause. ☐

LEVEL 4

- Shout at the listeners, to make sure everyone can hear. ☐
- Read loudly enough for everyone to hear, but without shouting. ☐
- Whisper, so nobody can hear any mistakes. ☐

LEVEL 5

- Read with natural expression, using punctuation to guide you. ☐
- Read every word in the same flat tone of voice. ☐
- Read with such over-exaggerated expression that it is hard to concentrate on the words themselves. ☐

Reading with expression

Good readers use clues in the text to help them to read with expression. Reading with the right expression makes you much more interesting to listen to and really brings your story to life.

Punctuation will tell you when to pause and whether you are reading an order or a question, for example.

Look at what characters say too, and the words the author uses to describe how they speak.

SATs practice

Match up the two halves of each sentence with a line. The second half will give you all the clues you need about how to read it out loud.

"Hurray! It's my birthday!"	shouted the boy.
"It's not fair!"	asked the lady.
"Would you like some cake?"	laughed the little girl.

"That's beautiful!"	enquired Matthew.
"This cake is stale,"	exclaimed Amy.
"Is David home?"	complained Mum, frowning.

"You'll never beat me!"	insisted Mum, angrily.
"Can I have my ball back?"	asked the boy, timidly.
"Go to bed, now!"	laughed the boy, spitefully.

Debating

Organising your ideas

In a debate, individuals or teams present opposing views and the audience decides which argument is stronger. Share your views on the topic with the other people on your team. If you have time, do some research in books or on the Internet, then organise your information into sensible arguments.

Remember, you might be asked to prepare a speech in favour of something you do not agree with. You need to think about the issues really carefully to do a good job.

SATs practice

Imagine you have been asked to prepare a speech in favour of only selling sweets to adults.

LEVEL 3 Write down **two** arguments in favour of the idea.

LEVEL 4 Write down a third argument in favour of the idea.

LEVEL 5 Write down a fourth argument in favour of the idea.

Thinking about your opponent

There are two sides to every debate. Good debaters think about the arguments their opponents are likely to use, so that they can be ready to argue back against them.

Listen carefully to what the other team say and make notes of things that you disagree with, so that you can respond to them when it is your turn to speak. It is not polite to interrupt, so use the time while they are speaking to think carefully about what their main points are. Then you can respond to those first.

SATs practice

Here are some notes in favour of using public transport instead of a car. Write down an argument that you could use to argue against each one.

Public bus services run regularly in most areas.

____

____

If everyone used public transport, the roads would be safer.

____

____

Public transport is better for the environment.

____

____

Speaking and listening skills

Interviewing people

You can find out about a topic or an event by interviewing people who know a lot about it, or were there. You have to ask the right questions to get the information you need. Including quotations from people will make your writing more lively and interesting. Just remember to use speech marks and say who is speaking.

SATs practice

Read these comments from the new world record-breaking speed reader, then answer the questions.

"It feels fantastic! I'm so thrilled to have beaten the record."

"I've always loved reading and I just noticed one day that I could read much faster than most people. After that, I was hooked."

"I read lots of books in the run-up to the event, to build up my speed."

LEVEL 3 Underline the quotation that would answer this question.

"How did it feel to beat the world speed-reading record?"

LEVEL 4 What question do you think the interviewer might have asked to get the final quotation?

____

____

LEVEL 5 Write down a question you could ask to find out about the speaker's future plans.

____

____

Taking notes

When you are interviewing someone, you often need to take notes of the key information. Your notes will remind you of the key facts later, when you are writing.

SATs practice

Read this interview and find the information needed to answer each question.

Interview

Interviewer:	Can you tell me why you decided to abolish school uniform?
Head teacher:	Yes. We have just moved into new buildings, so it seemed the right time for a fresh start. The children are very pleased.
Interviewer:	What do the parents of the children think about it?
Head teacher:	We have had a mixed response, but most of them are one hundred per cent behind us.
Interviewer:	Do you think other schools will follow your example?
Head teacher:	School uniform is an important part of many schools' identities, so I don't think many schools will follow our lead in the near future.

What do most parents think?

____

Why did the school decide to abolish school uniform?

____

What does the head teacher think other schools will do?

____

The language of books

On the cover

There are lots of special features on the cover of books that give us different information about the book. The cover of a book is the first thing you see, so it is often the thing that makes us decide to read a book.

Publishers, who produce and promote books, spend a lot of time and money making sure that the covers of their books grab readers' attention. They often have beautiful artwork and usually a blurb on the back, which is a short paragraph telling you a bit about the story and the characters, to make you want to read more.

Book covers also contain important information about the book, like who wrote and illustrated it, who published it and how much it costs. Covers also carry the book's unique ISBN (**I**nternational **S**tandard **B**ook **N**umber), which is used by booksellers and libraries to identify the book.

SATs practice

Write your own definition for each of these features.

LEVEL 3 The publisher

____

____

The blurb

____

____

The ISBN

____

Inside the book

The insides of books are full of special features you need to know about too. Many of them are designed to help readers to find the information they need, or to understand more about what they are reading.

SATs practice

Write down what each of these features does and where you would find it. You may need to look these up in a dictionary.

LEVEL 3 Picture captions

____

____

LEVEL 4 Index

____

____

LEVEL 5 Glossary

____

____

Description and imagery

Similes

Similes compare one thing with another, using the words *as* or *like*.

as quick as a flash

There are lots of 'well-known' similes, but you can always make up your own too. They are great for writing descriptions to help you to create atmosphere in your writing.

SATs practice

Pick a word from the box to complete each of these similes.

mule	thunder	ice

LEVEL 3 as cold as ____________

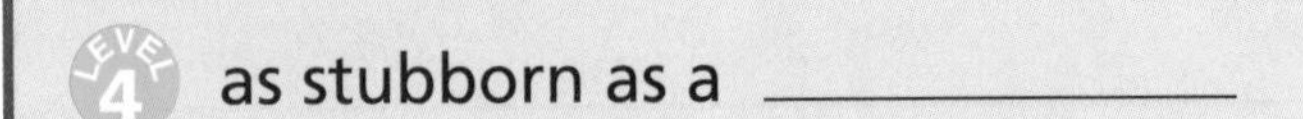

LEVEL 4 as stubborn as a ____________

LEVEL 5 a face like ____________

Metaphors

Metaphors describe something by saying that it is something else.

The dark was a silent enemy.

They are great for creating a vivid picture in your reader's mind.

SATs practice

Write down metaphors for these things.

LEVEL 3 the Sun ____________

LEVEL 4 a stormy sea ____________

LEVEL 5 a dark alleyway ____________

Personification

Personification is another type of imagery, where non-human things are described using human characteristics.

The Sun smiled down on us.

White clouds ambled across the blue sky.

SATs practice

Choose the best word from the brackets to complete each sentence.
Cross out the word you reject.

The empty windows (stared / winked) down from the crumbling walls.

The rusty hinges (whistled / screamed) as the gate swung open.

The volcano, which had (slumbered / snoozed) for years, was about to erupt.

Special effects

Alliteration

Alliteration is where lots of the words in a phrase begin with the same sound.

Tim took Tina to town on Tuesday.

You will often find it in poetry, so look out for it when you are asked to write about a poem. Alliteration is also what makes tongue-twisters so hard to say!

She sells seashells by the seashore.

The shells she sells are surely seashells.

So if she sells shells on the seashore,

I'm sure she sells seashore shells.

SATs practice

Think of a word to complete these alliterative sentences.

LEVEL 3 Baby Billy balanced ______________________ bricks.

LEVEL 4 Philip is famous for ______________________ fifty fossils.

LEVEL 5 ______________________ Cyril sipped steaming celery soup.

Onomatopoeia

Onomatopoeia words sound like what they descibe.

SATs practice

Write down two examples of onomatopoeia words to describe each of these things.

________________ ________________

________________ ________________

________________ ________________

Idioms

Idioms are not what they seem!

Idioms are phrases that don't mean what they seem to.

Feeling under the weather.

You cannot work out what an idiom means by looking at the meaning of the words – you just have to learn them. Each language has its own idioms and they are often one of the hardest things to learn when you are studying a new language. For example, *a pain in the neck* in English translates as *a real foot-breaker* in French!

SATs practice

Match up these idioms with their meanings.

LEVEL 3 fit as a fiddle — very easy

 a piece of cake — out of danger

 out of the woods — very healthy

Tired idioms

Some idioms are used so much that they have become rather boring. These are called clichés. It is best to avoid these in your writing.

It is raining cats and dogs.

SATs practice

Write these sentences again, using everyday language to replace the clichés.

LEVEL 3 It was raining cats and dogs all day.

____

____

LEVEL 4 His reaction was completely over the top.

____

____

LEVEL 5 At the end of the day, as long as everyone is safe, that is all that matters.

____

____

Ambiguity

What is ambiguity?

If the meaning of a sentence is unclear, we say that it is ambiguous. Often the meaning of a sentence is ambiguous, because it contains pronouns that could relate to more than one noun in the sentence.

The dog chased its tail until it was tired.

Who was tired – the dog or the tail?

Reading your writing carefully will help you to spot ambiguity before your teacher does!

SATs practice

Circle the sentence in each pair that is ambiguous.

LEVEL 3 Clare told her mum that she was hungry.

Clare told her dad that she was hungry.

LEVEL 4 The mother put the little girl to bed, because she was tired.

The boy fed the dog, because it was hungry.

LEVEL 5 The chick left the nest, because it was too small.

Clare asked her brother if he would play with her.

Making it clear

Often you can rewrite sentences to make the meaning clearer. Remember to watch out for pronouns that do not give enough information. Pay particular attention to very long sentences too, because it is much easier to get in a muddle with them.

SATs practice

Write these sentences again, so that they make sense.

LEVEL 3 The dog gobbled up the steak sandwich, because it looked lovely.

___

___

___

LEVEL 4 The policeman chased the boy, because he didn't have lights on his bike.

___

___

___

LEVEL 5 The baby didn't want its dinner, so Mum threw it in the bin.

___

___

___

Fiction and non-fiction

What is fiction?

Fiction is the name for 'made-up' stories. Fiction writing might be based on real people or events, but most of the detail comes from the writer's imagination.

Fiction writing tends to flow so that you can read it quickly to find out what happens next. Events follow on from each other, so you need to read it right through to understand it. Fiction authors often use a personal style of writing, so it seems as if they are talking directly to you.

SATs practice

Look at these pairs of statements about fiction text and circle the features that are true.

LEVEL 3 You read fiction all the way through, from start to finish.

You just read the bits of a fiction text that interest you.

LEVEL 4 Fiction contains lots of charts and diagrams, to present information to the reader.

Fiction for younger children might contain pictures, but for older children and adults it tends not to be illustrated.

LEVEL 5 Fiction authors often use an impersonal voice for describing things, e.g. *Bats are the only true flying mammals.*

Fiction authors often use a personal voice to describe things, e.g. *Bats swirled above them in the darkness.*

What is non-fiction?

Non-fiction is information writing, based on facts. Non-fiction books often have lots of illustrations and diagrams to help the reader to understand the content. They are arranged so that readers can just dip in for the information they need, without reading the whole book.

The style is usually quite impersonal, because the author is describing how things really are. There may be lots of technical words too, so non-fiction books often have a glossary at the back.

SATs practice

Say whether you think each of these statements about non-fiction is true or false.

LEVEL 3

Books that tell us about the natural world, science, history or sports are most likely to be non-fiction books. ______________

Non-fiction books are written using a personal voice. ______________

LEVEL 4

Readers need to read the whole of an information text, so they know what happens at the end. ______________

The information in non-fiction texts is usually organised into sections or chapters, to make it easier to find specific information. ______________

LEVEL 5

You can often work out what new or unfamiliar words in a non-fiction text mean by looking at what comes before or after them in the story. ______________

Non-fiction texts often use technical vocabulary that is specific to the topic. The meanings of these words are often given in a glossary. ______________

Authors and narrators

What is an author?

The author of a piece of writing is the person who wrote it. Fiction books usually only have one author, but non-fiction books can have two or more.

Sometimes, authors write in their own voice, talking about their own feelings and experiences. An example of this is autobiography, which is the story of someone's life, written by themselves.

SATs practice

LEVEL 3 What does an author do?

____

____

LEVEL 4 If a book has more than one author, is it more likely to be fiction or non-fiction?

____

LEVEL 5 Whose voice does the author use in an autobiography?

____

What does a narrator do?

The narrator is the storyteller in a fiction text.

Sometimes the narrator is a character in the story, and sometimes it is not.

Narrators who are characters in the story don't need to be people; sometimes they are animals, or even objects that are not alive at all!

SATs practice

These sentences all come from stories in which the narrator is a character. Who, or what, do you think the narrator is in each sentence?

The grown-up called Mummy lifted me gently from my cot and gave me a bottle of warm milk.

____

I scurried into a nearby dustbin, pursued by the family cat, who scrabbled through the rubbish, looking for me.

____

I felt my walls shake as the family left me, slamming my door behind them.

____

Life stories

Biographies

A biography is the story of a person's life, written by someone else. Good biographies are based mainly on fact, rather than fiction.

They are written in the third person.

Her first book was published in 1962.

SATs practice

Read the pairs of statements about biographies, then circle the statement that is true.

A biography is the story of someone's life that they write themselves.

A biography is the story of someone's life that is written by someone else.

LEVEL 4
The people in biographies are real, but all the details of their lives are fiction.

Good biographies are based mainly on fact.

Biographies are written in the first person, e.g. *I won my first gold medal at the age of 19.*

Biographies are written in the third person, e.g. *She won her first gold medal at the age of 19.*

Autobiographies

Autobiographies are also life stories, but they are written by the person whose life story they tell.

They are usually written in the first person.

I grew up in the countryside.

SATs practice

Decide whether you think each of these sentences comes from a biography or an autobiography.

She was seven when her family moved to England.

____

I always envied my sister, who went to ballet school.

____

My grandfather flew a fighter plane during World War II and used to entertain us with stories about it.

____

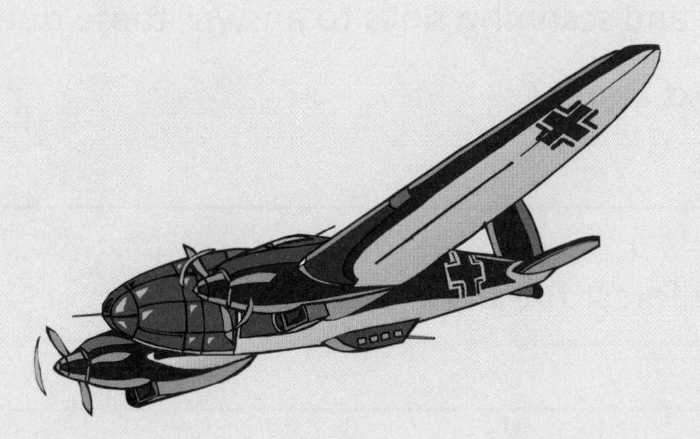

Comprehension skills

Reading skills

Comprehension tests are all about showing that you understand what you have read. There are different ways to read, that help you to understand different things about the text.

Skimming means reading quickly to work out what a text is about.

Once you have skimmed through the text, you scan or sweep through again, looking for key words that are linked to the questions.

SATs practice

I will never forget one camping holiday we went on, in the New Forest. It had been a hot, dry summer with very little rain, and we woke one morning to the smell of smoke throughout the campsite. A forest fire had broken out nearby and was heading our way! There was no time to take down the tent; we just had to get into the car and leave all of our things behind us. Luckily the wind direction changed so the fire never reached our tent, but it did destroy lots of the beautiful forest before the fire brigade put it out.

Use your skimming and scanning skills to answer these questions.

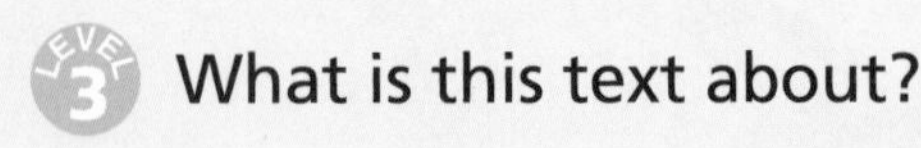

LEVEL 3 What is this text about?

____

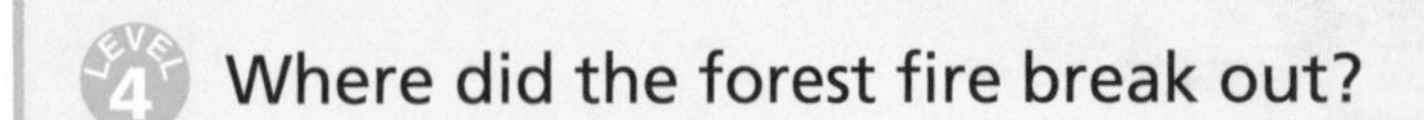

LEVEL 4 Where did the forest fire break out?

____

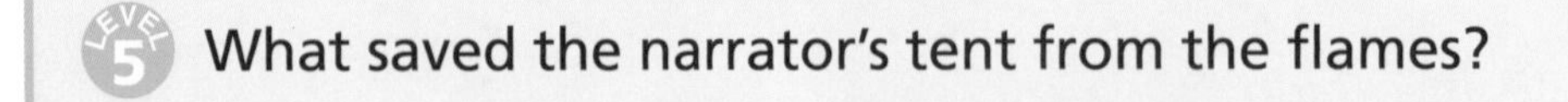

LEVEL 5 What saved the narrator's tent from the flames?

____

Reading questions

You need to look for key words in comprehension texts, but the questions contain key words too. Spotting the key words in a question will help you to find the information you need for the answer.

Read the text about slugs, then use the red key words in the questions to help you to answer them.

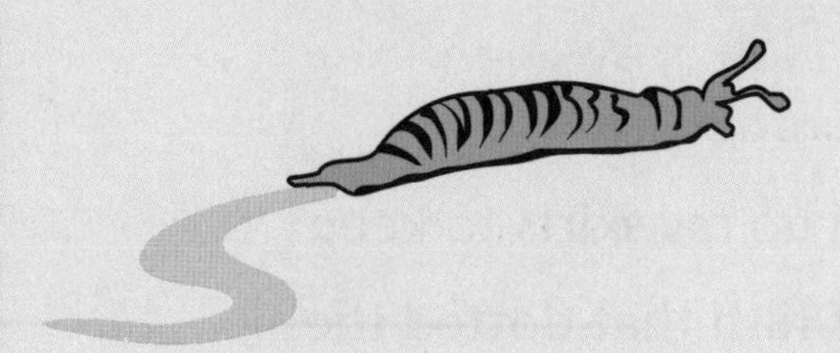

What do gardeners think of slugs?

Slugs are a gardener's enemy, feeding on the leaves of precious plants and leaving them full of holes. Slugs are a particular problem during wet weather, because they need moisture to survive. Some gardeners use chemicals to poison slugs, but many prefer to encourage natural predators like hedgehogs into their gardens instead.

LEVEL 3 What do slugs feed on?

____

LEVEL 4 What do slugs need to survive?

____

The hedgehog is a natural predator for slugs.
Why do you think some gardeners prefer to encourage this animal into their garden rather than using chemicals?

____

Using deduction

What is deduction?

Sometimes the answer to a comprehension question is right there in the text. Other times, you will need to use the evidence in the text, and your common sense, to find it. This is called deduction.

SATs practice

I pressed through the crowd, picking up my skirts to keep them out of the puddles and piles of filth that dotted the cobbled street. As the throng grew thicker I found my face scrubbed and scratched by the rough cloth of women's skirts as they surged forward, unaware of me pushing forward too, among the sea of legs. All of us hoped to catch a glimpse of the royal coach.

Use your deduction skills to answer these questions.

LEVEL 3 Who do you think the crowd is hoping to see?

____

LEVEL 4 Do you think the narrator is an adult, or a child?

____

LEVEL 5 Do you think the story is set in the past, or the present? Explain your answer.

____

____

Using empathy

To answer some questions, you will need to think about how a character might be feeling. This is called empathy.

SATs practice

Read this text, then use empathy to help you to answer the questions.

> Chris and Martin hesitated nervously on the threshold of the deserted house, before stepping inside. The boys split up to explore the empty rooms. Martin found himself in a large bedroom, empty except for dusty drapes at the window. He saw a movement in the shadows and froze. His throat was as dry as a bone but he managed to shout out to Chris, who fled down the stairs. Halfway down the hallway Chris thought of Martin, still upstairs, and stopped in his tracks.

LEVEL 3 Why is Martin's throat as dry as a bone?

____

LEVEL 4 Why do the boys hesitate on the way into the house?

____

LEVEL 5 Chris stops on the way out of the house. What do you think he will do next?

____

____

____

____

Reading and writing skills

Spotting clever techniques

You can use your reading skills to improve your writing. When you are reading, make a note of techniques that you think are particularly effective, so that you can adapt them for your own writing. Try to read as many different types of books as you can, to give you loads of great ideas for your own writing.

SATs practice

Underline the clever techniques in each of these sentences, then write the name of the technique in the box.

Amy stroked the cute kitten curled up on the cushion.

David's face was as white as a sheet.

The strawberry was a ruby nestling among the green leaves.

Improving your writing

You can often adapt techniques that you find in your reading, to use in your own writing. It is important that you change them and put them in your own style, though, to make them work for your writing.

SATs practice

Read these sentences, then adapt the technique to write your own sentences.

LEVEL 3 *Football is fast and fantastic!*

Use alliteration to write a sentence about your favourite sport.

____

____

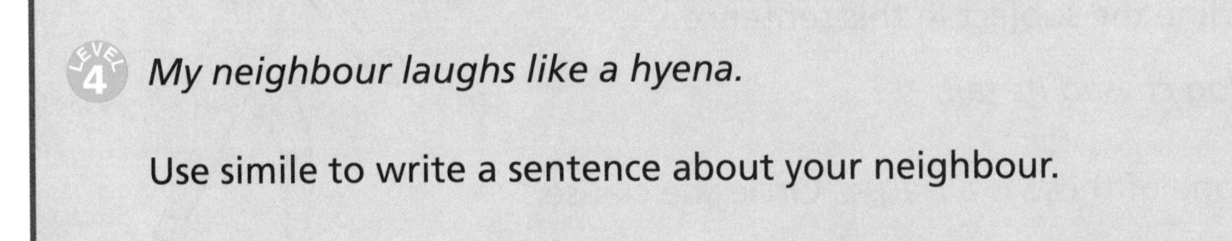

LEVEL 4 *My neighbour laughs like a hyena.*

Use simile to write a sentence about your neighbour.

____

____

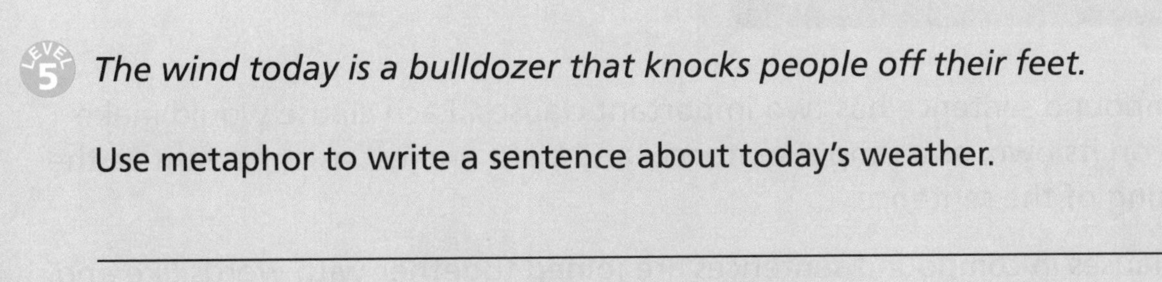

LEVEL 5 *The wind today is a bulldozer that knocks people off their feet.*

Use metaphor to write a sentence about today's weather.

____

____

Sentences

Simple sentences

A clause is part of a sentence and contains a subject and a verb.

Sarah was happy. A simple sentence contains one clause.

subject verb

SATs practice

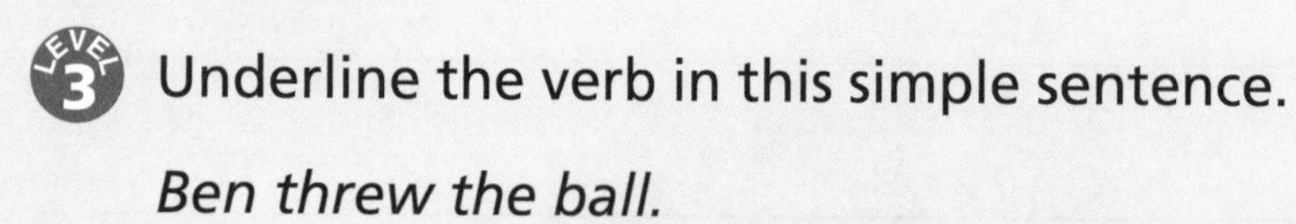

LEVEL 3 Underline the verb in this simple sentence.

Ben threw the ball.

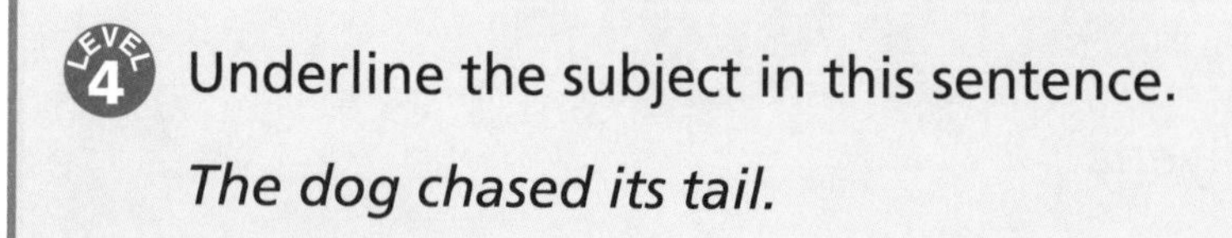

LEVEL 4 Underline the subject in this sentence.

The dog chased its tail.

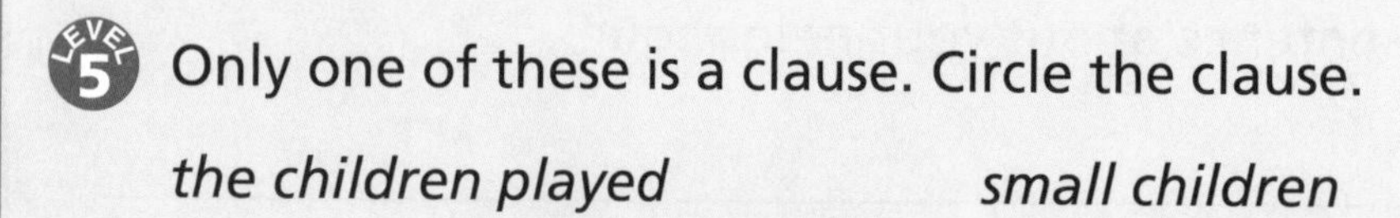

LEVEL 5 Only one of these is a clause. Circle the clause.

the children played *small children*

Compound sentences

A compound sentence has two important clauses. Each clause would make sense on its own, as a simple sentence, and both are just as important to the meaning of the sentence.

The clauses in compound sentences are joined together with words like *and, or, but* or *so*.

I bought a present and I gave it to Anna.

SATs practice

Underline the joining word in this sentence.

I was thirsty, so I made a drink.

Write out this sentence again, as two simple sentences.

I like pizza, but Andrew likes pasta.

Write this pair of simple sentences as one compound sentence.

I bought a stamp. I put it on my letter.

Complex sentences

Good writers use a variety of different sentences to make their writing interesting.

A complex sentence is based on a main clause, with one or more less important clauses, called subordinate clauses, added to it. The main clause would make sense on its own as a simple sentence, but subordinate clauses do not.

As he purred happily, the cat went to sleep.

subordinate clause (As he purred happily,) — **main clause** (the cat went to sleep.)

SATs practice

Underline the main clause in this complex sentence.

Chris ran to school, because he was late.

Underline the subordinate clause in this sentence.

As she licked her lips, Jane reached for biggest cake.

Which is the complex sentence in this group? Tick the correct answer.

When I saw that it was raining, I decided to take my umbrella. ☐

It was raining. ☐

It was raining, so I took my umbrella. ☐

Connectives

Cause and effect connectives

Connectives are words or phrases that join together parts of a sentence, or link two sentences together. They can work in different ways. Some connectives show that one thing happens because of, or in spite of, something else.

*We will go by car **if** it is raining.*

These are called cause and effect connectives and they help you to describe why things happen, or don't happen, in your writing.

SATs practice

Underline the cause and effect connective.

I was late for school, because my alarm clock was broken.

LEVEL 4 Underline the cause and effect connective.

My brother broke his arm the day before his birthday. Despite that, he had a great time.

LEVEL 5 Pick the best cause and effect connective from the box to complete this sentence.

because	if	so

I lost my bus money _______________ I had to walk home.

Time connectives

Connectives can also help us to describe *when* an event happened, or to put a series of events in order.

*I brushed my teeth **before** I went to bed.*

They can also explain whether something happened quickly or slowly.

*We were watching TV. **Suddenly**, all the lights went out.*

SATs practice

Pick a suitable time connective from the box to complete this sentence.

after before during

I looked both ways ______________________ crossing the road.

Underline the time connectives in this passage of writing.

The cat stretched before licking its paws.
Eventually it ambled over to its food bowl.

Pick time connectives from the box to complete this piece of writing.

Since Before During Suddenly All at once After While

____________ World War II, children were evacuated to the countryside to keep them safe. ______________ the war was over, they were allowed to go back home.

Contractions

Writing contractions

When two words are used together a lot, we can sometimes join them together by taking out some of the letters and replacing them with an apostrophe.

do not = don't

he is = he's

SATs practice

Write the contracted forms of these pairs of words.

I am ______________________

I had ______________________

we are ______________________

LEVEL 4 Write the contracted forms of these pairs of words.

they are ______________________

you will ______________________

is not ______________________

LEVEL 5 Write the contracted forms of these pairs of words.

will not ______________________

cannot ______________________

shall not ______________________

Using contractions

Contractions are used for dialogue, when characters are speaking, and for informal writing.

You don't usually see them in formal writing, so while you might use them in an email or letter to a friend, you would not in a letter to your school. Think carefully about the kind of writing you are doing before you use contractions.

SATs practice

Choose a phrase from the box to complete each sentence.

am	I'm	I'd	I would	won't	will not

LEVEL 3 " ____________ hungry!" complained Max.

LEVEL 4 Dear Susie, ____________ love to come to your party on Saturday. Love Amy

LEVEL 5 The management ____________ be held responsible for property lost or damaged. Explain your answer.

____

____

____

____

Possessive apostrophes

When to use possessive apostrophes

Possessive apostrophes show belonging.

To show that something belongs to somebody, you use an apostrophe followed by *s*.

a boy's football *the children's sweets*

For words that already end in *s*, you just add the apostrophe, without the *s*.

two boys' footballs

SATs practice

Add the possessive apostrophe to these sentences.

 I borrowed my brothers bike.

 We saw two rabbits tails disappearing into the undergrowth.

 The mens hard hats and shovels were in the van.

When not to use possessive apostrophes

Lots of people make mistakes with apostrophes and use them when there is no need to.

Sometimes people put them before the final *s* in plurals like *tomatoes* and *pianos*. These are sometimes called 'greengrocer's apostrophes'.

SATs practice

Underline the word with the correct apostrophe in each of these sentences.

Level 3: Having a party? Call Ken's mobile disco's!

Level 4: Tomato's are delicious, but this tomato's skin was very tough.

Level 5: The tornado's roar echo's around the valley.

Its and it's

If you want to say that something belongs to 'it', you don't use an apostrophe.

The bird sat on its nest.

That is because *its* is the contracted form of it is.

SATs practice

Choose *its* or *it's* to complete these sentences.

Level 3: The cat curled up on ________ cushion.

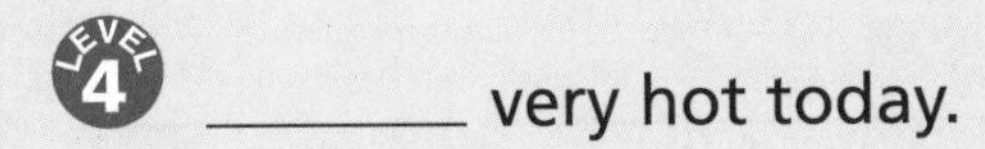
Level 4: ________ very hot today.

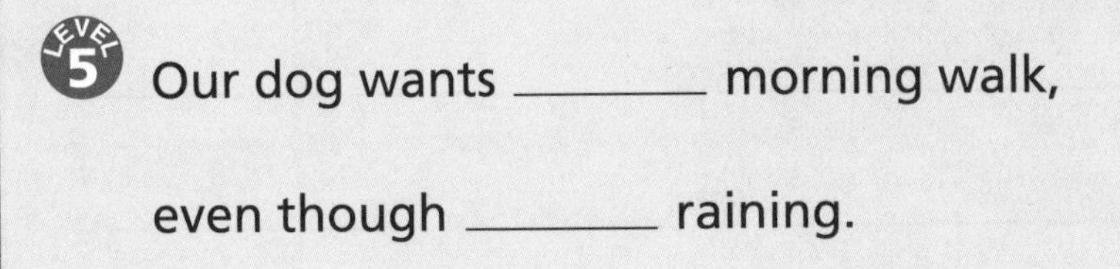
Level 5: Our dog wants ________ morning walk,

even though ________ raining.

Punctuation

Ending sentences

Most sentences end with a full stop, to show that the sentence has finished. Questions end with a question mark. Sentences that are giving an order, or delivering a surprise, often end with an exclamation mark.

When you have used a full stop, question mark or exclamation mark, you must start the next sentence with a capital letter.

SATs practice

 Use a full stop, question mark or exclamation mark to end this sentence.

Would you like to go to the cinema____

 Write a sentence that ends with a question mark.

____

____

 Write a sentence that ends with an exclamation mark.

____

____

Commas in sentences

Commas divide up parts of a sentence to make them clearer. They are often used to separate clauses in sentences. Commas tell readers to take a short pause when they are reading.

SATs practice

Add the commas to these sentences.

LEVEL 3 It was my birthday so I had a party.

LEVEL 4 The children ran off to play in the snow wearing their warmest clothes.

LEVEL 5 My pen pal who is called Sebastian comes from Poland.

Commas in lists

Commas can also be used to separate the items in lists. The only place you do not use a comma is before the final *and* in a list.

We ate doughnuts, flapjacks, fairy cakes and éclairs.

SATs practice

Add the commas to these sentences.

LEVEL 3 Chloe Eve Rachel and Grace came to my party.

LEVEL 4 I found a belt an apple core two bags and an old sock under my bed.

LEVEL 5 I needed to buy apples bread rolls plain flour and butter.

Colons and semi-colons

Colons

Colons are used to introduce lists or explanations in sentences.

Pancakes contain: flour, eggs and milk.

I was very tired: it was past midnight.

SATs practice

Add the colon to these sentences.

To grow a sunflower you will need a pot, some soil, water and sunflower seeds.

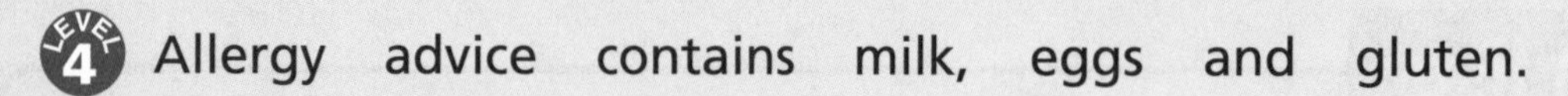

LEVEL 4 Allergy advice contains milk, eggs and gluten.

LEVEL 5 Katie was upset she had lost her favourite bag.

Semi-colons

Semi-colons are used to separate items in lists where the items are longer than one word each. They can sometimes also be used to separate clauses in sentences.

We need two eggs; half a bag of flour; half a kilo of sugar and a splash of milk.

I speak French; Sam speaks Spanish.

SATs practice

Cross out the incorrect semi-colon in the sentence.

I bought; a train set; some computer games; a chocolate selection box and a pair of stripy socks.

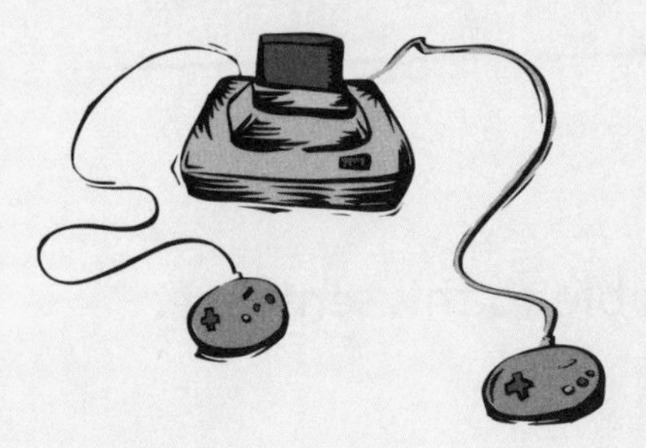

Add the semi-colon to this sentence.

I rescued the butterfly from the web it flew away.

Add the semi-colons to this sentence.

We packed a large tent sleeping bags a gas stove and spare tent pegs for our camping holiday.

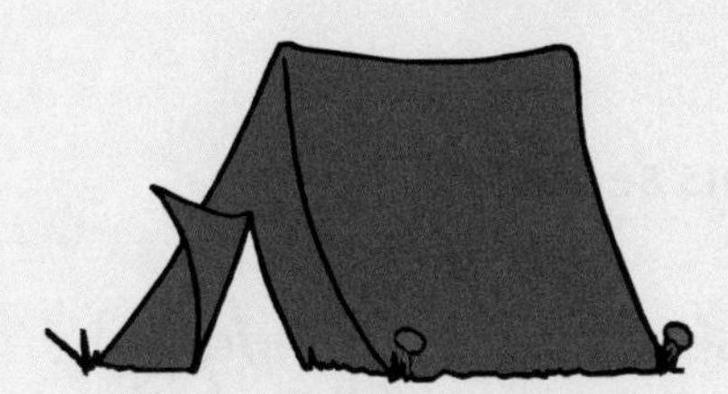

Writing about speech

Direct speech

Direct speech is the actual words that someone says. It is written inside speech marks and the first word always starts with a capital letter, even if it is in the middle of a sentence. The punctuation at the end of the speech always goes inside the speech marks.

SATs practice

 Underline the direct speech in this sentence.

"Why don't you switch off the TV and play outside instead?" suggested Mum.

LEVEL 4 Add the direct speech from the speech bubble to this sentence.

Ben said, ______________________________

____

 Add the speech marks and punctuation to this sentence.

Please can I have my ball back asked Kirsten politely.

Reported speech

Reported speech is where a writer tells the reader about what someone said, without using his or her actual words. We do not use speech marks for reported speech.

Laura said she would be back at teatime.

SATs practice

Rewrite these sentences as reported speech.

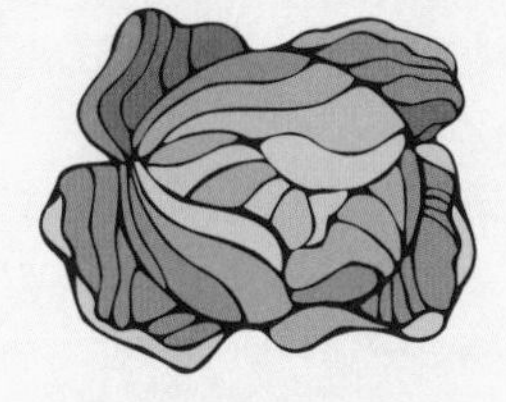

"I hate cabbage!" said the boy.

____

The teacher explained, "We are going on a trip to the museum next week."

____

____

"Please can we have a kitten; they are so sweet!" pleaded Mandy.

____

____

Plurals

Adding *s*

Plural means more than one of something. Usually you can just add *s* to a word to make it plural.

dog   *dogs*   *hat*   *hats*

If a word already ends in *s*, or in *x*, *zz*, *ch*, or *sh*, you have to add *es* instead.

dress   *dresses*   *box*   *boxes*

SATs practice

Write down the plurals of these words.

LEVEL 3 cat ________   house ________   tree ________

LEVEL 4 caterpillar ________   watch________   road ________

LEVEL 5 bush ________   match ________   bus ________

Words ending in *y*

To make the plural of words that end in a vowel followed by *y*, you just add *s*.

key   *keys*

If the word ends in a consonant then *y*, you have to take the *y* off and add *ies*.

baby   *babies*

SATs practice

Underline the correct spelling for each plural.

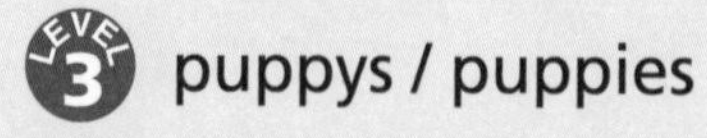

LEVEL 3 puppys / puppies   toies / toys

LEVEL 4 nappys / nappies   plays / plaies   trolleys / trollies

LEVEL 5 dayes / days   donkeys / donkies

boies / boys   ladies / ladys

English answer booklet

SPEAKING AND LISTENING

READING ALOUD

PAGE 4 What makes good reading?

Ticked answers should be:

3 Read at a natural pace, letting punctuation help the reader to decide when to pause.

4 Read loudly enough for everyone to hear, but without shouting.

5 Read with natural expression, with punctuation to guide you.

PAGE 5 Reading with expression

Complete sentences should be:

3 "Hurray! It's my birthday!" laughed the little girl.
"It's not fair!" shouted the boy.
"Would you like some cake?" asked the lady.

4 "That's beautiful!" exclaimed Amy.
"This cake is stale," complained Mum, frowning.
"Is David home?" enquired Matthew.

5 "You'll never beat me!" laughed the boy, spitefully.
"Can I have my ball back?" asked the boy, timidly.
"Go to bed, now!" insisted Mum, angrily.

DEBATING

PAGE 6 Organising your ideas

Many answers are possible, but may include:
Sweets are bad for children's teeth.
Children waste too much pocket money on sweets.
It would be better for parents to decide how many sweets to buy for their children.
Children would then have more pocket money to spend on other things.
Children eat too many sweets in between meals.

PAGE 7 Thinking about your opponent

Many answers are possible, but may include:

3 In some areas, buses run only once or twice a day.

4 Many people do not feel safe using public transport, especially at night.

5 Many buses run with only a few passengers, and this is worse for the environment than if they travelled in a car.

SPEAKING AND LISTENING SKILLS

PAGE 8 Interviewing people

3 "It feels fantastic! I'm so thrilled to have beaten the record."

4 "How did you prepare for the event?"

5 "Do you have any plans to take part in future speed-reading events?"

PAGE 9 Taking notes

3 They are one hundred per cent behind it.

4 They had just moved into new buildings, so it seemed the right time for a fresh start.

5 They will not follow their lead.

READING

THE LANGUAGE OF BOOKS

PAGE 10 On the cover

3 The publisher is the company that prints and promotes a book.

4 The blurb is information on the back of a book, which gives an idea of what the story is about.

5 Books have a unique ISBN number which is used by publishers, libraries and booksellers to identify the book.

PAGE 11 Inside the book

3 Picture captions describe what is in a picture. They are usually found below the picture.

4 The index is an alphabetical list of the topics in a non-fiction book, together with page numbers for each topic. The index is found at the back of the book.

5 A glossary is an alphabetical list of difficult or technical words in a non-fiction book, together with their definitions. Glossaries are found at the back of a book.

DESCRIPTION AND IMAGERY

PAGE 12 Similes

3 as cold as ice

4 as stubborn as a mule

5 a face like thunder

PAGE 12 Metaphors

Many answers are possible, but could include:

3 the Sun was a fiery disc.

4 a stormy sea is a wild beast.

5 a dark alleyway is a dragon's throat.

PAGE 13 Personification

3 stared

4 screamed

5 slumbered

SPECIAL EFFECTS

PAGE 14 Alliteration

Many answers are possible, but could include:

3 Baby Billy balanced blue bricks.

4 Philip is famous for finding fifty fossils.

5 Silly Cyril sipped steaming celery soup.

PAGE 15 Onomatopoeia

Many answers are possible, but could include:

3 bang, pop

4 rustle, crunch

5 screech, howl

IDIOMS

PAGE 16 Idioms are not what they seem!

3 fit as a fiddle means very healthy

4 a piece of cake means very easy

5 out of the woods means out of danger

PAGE 17 Tired idioms

Answers may vary.

3 It was raining hard all day.

4 He completely over reacted.

5 In the end, the safety of everyone is the most important thing.

AMBIGUITY

PAGE 18 What is ambiguity?

Circled answers should be:

3 Clare told her mum that she was hungry.

4 The mother put the little girl to bed, because she was tired.

5 The chick left the nest, because it was too small.

PAGE 19 Making it clear

Exact answers may vary, but could include:

3 The steak sandwich looked lovely, so the dog gobbled it up.

4 The boy didn't have lights on his bike, so the policeman chased him.

5 Mum threw the baby's dinner in the bin, because the baby didn't want it.

FICTION AND NON-FICTION

PAGE 20 What is fiction?

Circled answers should be:

3 You read fiction all the way through, from start to finish.

4 Fiction for younger children might contain pictures, but for older children and adults it tends not to be illustrated.

5 Fiction authors often use a personal voice to describe things, e.g. Bats swirled above them in the darkness.

PAGE 21 What is non-fiction?

3 true, false

4 false, true

5 false, true

AUTHORS AND NARRATORS

PAGE 22 What is an author?

3 The author is the writer of the book.

4 non-fiction

5 their own voice

PAGE 23 What does a narrator do?

3. a baby
4. a mouse or rat
5. a house

LIFE STORIES

PAGE 24 Biographies

Circled answers should be:

3. A biography is the story of someone's life that is written by someone else.
4. Good biographies are based mainly on fact.
5. Biographies are written in the third person, e.g. She won her first gold medal at the age of 19.

PAGE 25 Autobiographies

3. biography
4. autobiography
5. autobiography

COMPREHENSION SKILLS

PAGE 26 Reading skills

3. a forest fire
4. New Forest
5. The wind changed direction.

PAGE 27 Reading questions

3. the leaves of plants
4. moisture
5. Because it is a more environmentally friendly way than using chemicals that damage plants as well.

USING DEDUCTION

PAGE 28 What is deduction?

3. a king, queen or other member of the royal family
4. a child
5. The story is set in the past, because the girl has to pick up her skirts to keep them out of the dirt, and girls do not usually wear long skirts today.
   Also, the stories mention piles of filth on the streets, which implies that people do not have dustbins.

PAGE 29 Using empathy

3. because he is scared
4. because they are not sure what they will find inside
5. go back for Martin

READING AND WRITING SKILLS

PAGE 30 Spotting clever techniques

3. alliteration
4. simile
5. metaphor

PAGE 31 Improving your writing

Many answers are possible.

WRITING

SENTENCES

PAGE 32 Simple sentences

3. Ben threw the ball.
4. The dog chased its tail.
5. the children played is the clause

PAGE 33 Compound sentences

3. I was thirsty, so I made a drink.
4. I like pizza. Andrew likes pasta.
5. I bought a stamp, then I put it on my letter.
   OR I bought a stamp and I put it on my letter.

PAGE 33 Complex sentences

3. Chris ran to school, because he was late.
4. As she licked her lips, Jane reached for the biggest cake.
5. The complex sentence is: When I saw that it was raining, I decided to take my umbrella.

CONNECTIVES

PAGE 34 Cause and effect connectives

3. I was late for school, because my alarm clock was broken.
4. My brother broke his arm the day before his birthday. Despite that, he had a great time.
5. I lost my bus money so I had to walk home.

PAGE 35 Time connectives

3. I looked both ways before crossing the road.
4. The cat stretched before licking its paws. Eventually it ambled over to its food bowl.
5. During World War II, children were evacuated to the countryside to keep them safe. After the war was over, they were allowed to go back home.

CONTRACTIONS

PAGE 36 Writing contractions

3. I'm, I'd, we're
4. they're, you'll, isn't
5. won't, can't, shan't

PAGE 37 Using contractions

3. I'm
4. I'd
5. will not (This is because it is a piece of formal writing).

POSSESSIVE APOSTROPHES

PAGE 38 When to use possessive apostrophes

3. I borrowed my brother's bike.
4. We saw two rabbits' tails disappearing into the undergrowth.
5. The men's hard hats and shovels were in the van.

PAGE 39 When not to use possessive apostrophes

3. Having a party? Call Ken's mobile disco's!
4. Tomato's are delicious, but this tomato's skin was very tough.
5. The tornado's roar echo's around the valley.

PAGE 39 Its and it's

3. its
4. It's
5. its, it's

PUNCTUATION

PAGE 40 Ending sentences

3. Would you like to go to the cinema?
4. Many answers are possible, but the sentence must be a question.
5. Many answers are possible, but the sentence must deliver an order or a surprise.

PAGE 41 Commas in sentences

3. It was my birthday, so I had a party.
4. The children ran off to play in the snow, wearing their warmest clothes.
5. My pen pal, who is called Sebastian, comes from Poland.

PAGE 41 Commas in lists

3. Chloe, Eve, Rachel and Grace came to my party.
4. I found a belt, an apple core, two bags and an old sock under my bed.
5. I needed to buy apples, bread rolls, plain flour and butter.

COLONS AND SEMI-COLONS

PAGE 42 Colons

3. To grow a sunflower you will need: a pot, some soil, water and sunflower seeds.
4. Allergy advice: contains milk, eggs and gluten
5. Katie was upset: she had lost her favourite bag.

PAGE 43 Semi-colons

3. I bought a train set; some computer games; a chocolate selection box and a pair of stripy socks.
4. I rescued the butterfly from the web; it flew away.
5. We packed a large tent; sleeping bags; a gas stove and spare tent pegs, for our camping holiday.

WRITING ABOUT SPEECH

PAGE 44 Direct speech

3. "Why don't you switch off the TV and play outside instead?" suggested Mum.
4. Ben said, "This book is so good, I can't put it down!"
5. "Please can I have my ball back?" asked Kirsten politely.

PAGE 45 Reported speech

3. The boy said that he hated cabbage.
4. The teacher explained that we were going on a trip to the museum next week.
   OR The teacher explained that they were going on a trip to the museum next week.
5. Mandy pleaded for a kitten, because she thought they were sweet.

PLURALS

PAGE 46 Adding *s*

3. cats, houses, trees
4. caterpillars, watches, roads
5. bushes, matches, buses

PAGE 46 Words ending in *y*
3 puppies, toys
4 nappies, plays, trolleys
5 days, donkeys, boys, ladies

PAGE 47 Words ending in *f*
3 leaves
4 cliffs, loaves
5 wolves, roofs, hooves or hoofs

PAGE 47 Words ending in *o*
3 potatoes
4 igloos, tomatoes
5 Many answers are possible, but could include: photos, kilos, heroes, echoes

NOUNS

PAGE 48 Common nouns
3 The tulips were red.
4 Daniel kicked the ball.
5 Susie caught the bus, because she was late.

PAGE 48 Proper nouns
Circled answers should be:
3 Claire's
4 Thomas, Spain
5 Tuesday, London, Tamara

PAGE 49 Collective nouns
3 a herd of cows
4 a shoal or school of fish
5 Many answers are possible, for instance: a chatter of children

PRONOUNS

PAGE 50 Using pronouns
3 I asked Olivia if she would like to come to tea.
4 Sophie stroked the cat, but it scratched her.
5 Mum called for Dad to catch the spider, but he was out, so she had to catch it.

PAGE 51 Choosing pronouns
3 it
4 they, us
5 he, she, him

VERBS

PAGE 52 Active and passive verbs
3 active
4 passive
5 The window had been broken

PAGE 53 Choosing verbs
Answers may vary.
3 The angry man yelled at us.
4 The girls giggled at the joke.
5 My sister stormed out of the room in a huff.

VERB TENSES

PAGE 54 What is a tense?
3 present tense
4 present
5 Annabel is afraid, because it is dark.

PAGE 55 Writing past tense verbs
3 Daisy painted a picture.
4 Mum baked a cake for my cousin's wedding.
5 Dad wondered where he had left his keys.

PAGE 55 Irregular past tense verbs
3 slept, went
4 caught, found, lost
5 brought, thought, ran, drew

ADVERBS

PAGE 56 What is an adverb?
3 The little girl smiled brightly.
4 The boy bravely climbed the tree to rescue the stranded cat.
5 The mouse sniffed the cheese hungrily and nibbled the edge greedily.

PAGE 57 Choosing adverbs
Many answers are possible, but might include:
3 angrily
4 cheerfully
5 dreamily

NOUNS AND VERBS

PAGE 58 Verb parts
3 he walks
4 you sleep, it sleeps
5 you are, he is, it is, we are

PAGE 59 Matching nouns and verbs
3 love
4 sleeps, sleep
5 go, goes, travel

ADJECTIVES

PAGE 60 What are adjectives?
3 The brave knight rode into battle on his beautiful horse.
4 The creepy cave gaped like an enormous, toothless mouth.
5 The jet-black crow swooped across the sunny garden like a sinister shadow, blotting out the dazzling sunshine.

PAGE 60 Comparative and superlative adjectives
3 smaller
4 most
5 least

PAGE 61 Choosing adjectives
Answers may vary.
3 The elephant was enormous.
4 I am reading a fascinating book about dinosaurs.
5 My mum was really delighted when I won first prize in the writing competition.

HOMOPHONES

PAGE 62 What are homophones?
3 two or to
4 wear or ware
5 stairs

PAGE 63 Choosing the right homophone
3 floor
4 their
5 pears, great

SPELLING RULES FOR SUFFIXES

PAGE 64 Simple suffix addition
3 playful, enjoyable, sadly
4 endless, agreeable, properly
5 foreseeable, carefree, sincerely

PAGE 65 Changing *y* to *i*
3 windier, beautiful
4 friendlier, silliness, reliable
5 plentiful, crazily, shyness, silkiness

SYNONYMS

PAGE 66 Looking for new words
3 gobbled
4 glowed
5 enough

PAGE 66 Adding variety
Many answers are possible.
3 "Have you done your homework yet?" asked James. "No, not yet," replied Max.
4 The girls were afraid when they heard the noise, because they were terrified of the dark.
5 Jenny scribbled out what she had written, then scrawled another note.

PAGE 67 Choosing synonyms
3 hit
4 smiled
5 arranged

ANTONYMS

PAGE 68 What are antonyms?
3 wide → narrow
warm → cool
short → long
4 leave → arrive
asleep → awake
empty → full
5 sell
pupil
child
found

PAGE 69 Using antonyms
Answers may vary, but may include:
3 tiny
4 patient
5 set

HOW WRITERS CREATE MOOD

PAGE 70 Clever techniques
3 cramped
4 trickled
5 Answers may vary, but might include snake

PAGE 71 Combining techniques
Many answers are possible, but might include:
3 The door was made of worn, withered wood.
4 The heavy old door squeaked open slowly.
5 The windows were eyes, blankly staring.

HOW ENGLISH IS ENGLISH?

PAGE 72 Loanwords

❸ glitzy
❹ salon, garage
❺ balcony, opera, violin, orchestra

PAGE 73 Dialect

❸ food
❹ bonfire, best
❺ money, father

INSTRUCTIONS

PAGE 74 What are instructions?

❸ a recipe
❹ How to build your chest of drawers
❺ Do not walk on the grass.

PAGE 75 Breaking down the task

❸ **1** Buy five fresh oranges.
2 Ask an adult to slice each orange in half.
3 Squeeze the orange halves, to extract the juice.
4 Chill the juice before drinking.
❹ Many answers are possible, but could include:
How to make salt crystals
❺ Stir the mixture until the salt has dissolved.

PERSUASIVE WRITING

PAGE 76 Types of persuasive writing

❸ in a fairy tale
on a road sign
❹ a leaflet about a castle, from the tourist information centre
❺ newspaper adverts
radio adverts
Internet adverts

PAGE 76 Choosing language

❸ tallest, eagerly, thrill, lucky
❹ tallest
❺ Answers will vary:
The theme park is huge, with a fantastic variety of rides, so there is something for everyone!

PAGE 77 Setting out your writing

❸ 'Special occasions' is a sub-heading
❹ newest and biggest
❺ Answers may vary, but might include: 'Facilities' or 'Exciting Features'.

REPORTS

PAGE 78 What are reports?

❸ false
❹ true
❺ true

PAGE 79 Planning reports

❸ Beech and bracken should be circled green.
Pheasants and foxes should be circled red.
Stag beetles and wood ants should be circled blue.
❹ badgers should be circled red; nettles should be circled green; spiders should be circled blue.
❺ Answers may vary, but animals, plants and mini-beasts should be labelled using the correct colours.

ADDING INFORMATION

PAGE 80 Parenthesis

❸ The bus (which was already late) sped right past us, without stopping.
❹ I will pass my English test (I hope!).
❺ My mum (who was late for work) hurried us off to school.

PAGE 81 Footnotes

❸ false
❹ a glossary
❺ Footnotes give extra information about the text on the page, and may provide the definitions of difficult words.

RECOUNTS

PAGE 82 Features of recounts

❸ The hairdresser cutting the girl's hair.
❹

❺ The girl went into the hairdressers. The hairdresser cut her hair. The girl saw her new hairstyle. She decided to hide it!

PAGE 83 Using time connectives

❸ We found a stray cat in our garden. Mum rang the local animal rescue centre, and afterwards we put up posters around the town. After that we waited for her owners to get in touch. Eventually, we realised that nobody was going to claim her, so in the end we decided to adopt her.
❹ first ➜ to begin with
then ➜ next
in the end ➜ finally
suddenly ➜ all at once
❺ I was on my way to school when I saw a wallet lying in the gutter. After I had made sure its owner wasn't nearby, I took the wallet to the police station. Next, I had to fill in a form, and then a policeman drove me to school in a police car. Later that day the police rang to say that a man had collected his wallet, and left a reward for me.

CHARACTERS

PAGE 84 What is a character?

❸ Danny and Violet
❹ mice
❺ Violet

PAGE 85 Developing characters

❸ Grandma
❹ the wolf
❺ Little Red Riding Hood

OPENINGS AND ENDINGS

PAGE 86 Story starters

❸ What is in the box?
❹ a puppy; quivering, whining
❺ Answers may vary.
"Go on, birthday girl, have a look inside," said Dad, smiling mischievously down at the box on the doorstep.

PAGE 87 Ending your story

Many answers are possible.
❸ The puppy is found safe and well.
❹ Another neighbour sees the boy let the dog out, and the boy gets into trouble.
❺ Many answers are possible.

PLOTTING

PAGE 88 Clustering ideas

❸ Many answers are possible.
❹ Join numbered arrows:
1 girl on holiday finds trap door leading to secret beach and sees an old pirate ship
2 overhears pirates plotting to take over village – nobody believes her
3 finds book in library and realises the pirate attack really did take place, but 200 years before
4 befriends son of the librarian and takes him to the beach to see the ship
❺ Many answers are possible.

PAGE 89 Stages in a story plan

❸ opening
❹ Many answers are possible, but might include: They cannot find an exact match for the vase at the shop.
❺ Many answers are possible, but might include: The children own up for the broken vase, but it turns out that their grandmother hated the vase anyway.

POETRY

PAGE 90 Kennings

❸ the sea
❹ Many answers are possible. An example is fish-storer.
❺ Many answers are possible.

PAGE 91 List poems

❸ Many answers are possible. An example is the smell of sunscreen.
❹ Many answers are possible. An example is flower-filled air.
❺ Many answers are possible.

Words ending in *f*

When a singular word ends in *f*, you usually take off the *f* and add *ves* to make the plural.

calf *calves*

Roof is among the exceptions to this rule. You just add *s* to make it plural.

With words that end in *ff*, you just add *s* to make the plural.

puff of smoke *puffs of smoke*

SATs practice

Write down the plurals of these words.

 leaf ______________

 cliff ______________ loaf ______________

 wolf ______________ roof ______________ hoof ______________

Words ending in *o*

With most words ending in *o*, you have to add *es* to make the plural.

There are some exceptions, though. The plurals of words which end in *oo*, and some which end in *o*, just end in *s*.

zoos *pianos*

A few can be spelt *s* or *es*.

mangos *mangoes*

SATs practice

Write down the plurals of these words.

 potato ____________________

 igloo ____________________ tomato ____________________

 Write down one word that ends in *os* and one that ends in *oes*.

_________________________ _________________________

Nouns

Common nouns

Nouns are words that name things. Common nouns name ordinary things.

flower, tree, bag, man

They start with lower case letters, unless they are at the beginning of a sentence.

SATs practice

Underline the common nouns in these sentences.

 The tulips were red.

 Daniel kicked the ball.

 Susie caught the bus, because she was late.

Proper nouns

Proper nouns name people and places, and important things like the days of the week and the months of the year. They always start with a capital letter, wherever they appear in a sentence.

Eve Bristol Wednesday March

SATs practice

Circle the proper nouns in these sentences, which should begin with a capital letter.

 It is claire's birthday today.

 My friend thomas is on holiday in spain.

 On tuesday I am going to london with tamara.

Collective nouns

Collective nouns name groups of things. There are different collective nouns for different things.

a pack of cards *a swarm of bees*

SATs practice

Complete these collective nouns.

a ______________ of cows

a ______________ of fish

Make up your own collective noun for a group of children.

____

Pronouns

Using pronouns

Pronouns like *I, she, me* and *her* are words that can replace nouns in a sentence. They save you from having to keep using the same noun again and again.

SATs practice

Underline the pronouns in these sentences.

Laura asked Olivia if she would like to come to tea.

LEVEL 4 Sophie stroked the cat, but it scratched her.

Mum called for Dad to catch the spider, but he was out, so she had to catch it.

Choosing pronouns

There are different pronouns to replace different nouns. Some help you to write about yourself, some describe males, some females, and others are used for groups.

*Kate was late, so we waited for **her**.*

*The twins play in the school football team, because **they** are great at football.*

SATs practice

Pick the correct pronoun to complete each sentence.

LEVEL 3

they	she	it

I blew up the balloon but ______________ burst.

LEVEL 4

them	they	we	us	it	she

My cousins are coming to visit and ______________ will stay with ______________ for two weeks.

LEVEL 5

she	he	them	us	it	him	her

Dawn ate her brother's sweets when ______________ wasn't looking, so ______________ had to buy ______________ some more.

Verbs

Active and passive verbs

Verbs are words that describe actions. Active verbs describe what someone or something is doing.

Robbie drank the milk.

Passive verbs focus on what is being done, rather than who is doing it. A sentence with passive verbs tells you about the thing or person that something is happening to. They do not always tell you who or what is performing the action.

The milk had all been used.

SATs practice

Decide whether each sentence contains an active or a passive verb.

Faith brushed her hair. ____________

The food was not cooked thoroughly. ____________

Rewrite the sentence with a passive verb.

Connor kicked the ball too hard and broke the window.

____

____

Choosing verbs

All sentences contain a verb, but some verbs are more useful than others. Verbs like *run, talk* and *sleep* are used all the time and can sound a bit boring. Thinking of more powerful alternatives, like *sprint, chatter* and *doze,* will make your writing more interesting.

SATs practice

Write these sentences again, with a more powerful verb.

LEVEL 3 The angry man shouted at us.

____

____

The girls laughed at the joke.

____

____

My sister walked out of the room, in a huff.

____

____

Verb tenses

What is a tense?

The tense of a verb tells us when something happens.

The past tense means it has already happened.

I walked to school.

The present tense means it is happening now.

I am walking to school.

Be careful not to keep changing tenses in your writing. It makes it very hard for your readers to work out when things happen in the story!

SATs practice

Decide whether this sentence is written in the past or present tense. Tick the correct box.

Alex is hungry.

present tense ☐ past tense ☐

Decide whether this sentence takes place in the past or the present. Tick the correct box.

The teacher is angry, because the children forgot their homework.

present ☐ past ☐

This sentence is written in the past tense. Write it again in the present tense.

Annabel was afraid, because it was dark.

____

Writing past tense verbs

Lots of past tense verbs end in *ed*.

wash ➜ *washed*

SATs practice

Write out these present tense sentences again, in the past tense.

LEVEL 3 Daisy paints a picture.

____

LEVEL 4 Mum bakes a cake for my cousin's wedding.

____

LEVEL 5 Dad wonders where he has left his keys.

____

Irregular past tense verbs

Some past tense verbs are spelt quite differently from the present tense version. You need to remember these separately, because most of them do not follow a pattern.

write ➜ *wrote*   *speak* ➜ *spoke*

SATs practice

LEVEL 3 Choose the past tense for these verbs. Tick the correct box.

sleep ➜ sleeped ☐ slept ☐   go ➜ went ☐ goed ☐

LEVEL 4 Write down the past tense of these verbs.

catch ________ find ________ lose ________

LEVEL 5 Write down the past tense of these verbs.

bring ________ think ________ run ________

draw ________

Adverbs

What is an adverb?

Adverbs describe verbs.

The dog ate greedily.

In this sentence, the adverb *greedily* describes the verb *ate*. It tells us more about how the dog ate.

Many adverbs end in *ly*, which makes them easier to spot in a sentence.

SATs practice

Underline the adverbs in these sentences.

LEVEL 3 The little girl smiled brightly.

LEVEL 4 The boy bravely climbed the tree to rescue the stranded cat.

LEVEL 5 The mouse sniffed the cheese hungrily and nibbled the edge greedily.

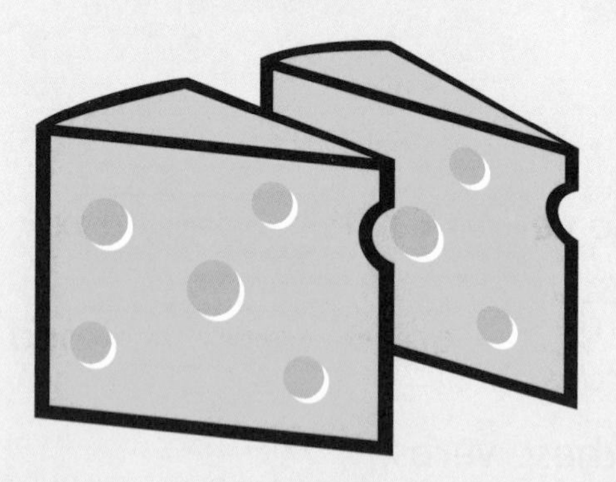

Choosing adverbs

Adverbs can help you to describe exactly how something is done. They help to create a picture in your reader's mind.

Adverbs work best when you team them up with really strong verbs.

*The boy **walked slowly** to school.*

OR

*The boy **sauntered reluctantly** to school.*

SATs practice

Think of a suitable adverb to complete these sentences.

The man shouted ____________________ at the howling cat.

"Hello," exclaimed the shopkeeper, ____________________ .

"It's beautiful!" murmured the woman, ____________________ .

Nouns and verbs

Verb parts

Verbs describe actions. Different parts of present tense verbs are used to describe what different people, things and groups are doing.

I run

she runs

we run

It is important to use the right part of the verb to describe what is happening in your writing.

SATs practice

Add the missing parts of the present tense verb.

LEVEL 3 I walk

he ____________

they walk

LEVEL 4 I sleep

you ____________

it ____________

we sleep

LEVEL 5 I am

you ____________

he ____________

it ____________

we ____________

Matching nouns and verbs

When you are writing a sentence, you have to make sure that the part of the verb you use matches the noun or pronoun in your sentence.

I wait for the bus.

She waits for the bus.

SATs practice

Pick the right verbs to complete these sentences.

loves   love

I ________ to eat Italian food.

the top bunk

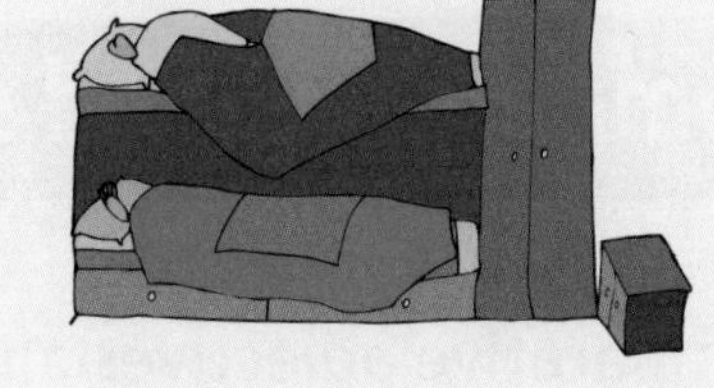

ottom bunk.

vel

unior school and

he upper school in

h ________

South Lambeth Library
www.lambeth.gov.uk/libraries
Tel: 020 7926 0705

Borrowed Items 20/12/2019 11:51
XXXX1936

Item Title	Due Date
* Dragon magic	10/01/2020 00:00
* Night I met Father Christmas	10/01/2020 00:00
* Cat who got carried away	10/01/2020 00:00
* Frogs do not like dragons	10/01/2020 00:00
* Stepmonster	10/01/2020 00:00
* Dinosaurs	10/01/2020 00:00
* Architecture according to pigeons	10/01/2020 00:00
* English.	10/01/2020 00:00
Oxford Reading Tree: Stage 15: TreeTops Non-Fict	07/01/2020 00:00
Save pudding wood.	07/01/2020 00:00
KS2 English SATs.	07/01/2020 00:00
Counting on Katherine	07/01/2020 00:00

* Indicates items borrowed today
Thank you for using self service

Adjectives

What are adjectives?

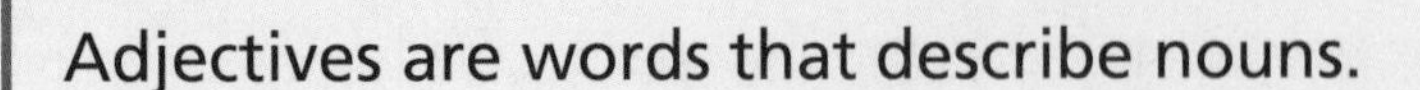

Adjectives are words that describe nouns.

The dog wagged its tail. *The **black** dog wagged its **fluffy** tail.*

SATs practice

Underline the adjectives in these sentences.

The brave knight rode into battle on his beautiful horse.

The creepy cave gaped like an enormous, toothless mouth.

The jet-black crow swooped across the sunny garden like a sinister shadow, blotting out the dazzling sunshine.

Comparative and superlative adjectives

Comparative adjectives allow you to compare one thing with another.

*My cake is **bigger** than yours.* *I am **more excited** than you.*

Superlative adjectives describe the most of a particular quality that something can be.

*Greg's cake is the **biggest** of all.* *Alice is the **most excited** of all of us.*

SATs practice

Add a suitable word to complete each sentence.

Charlie's kitten is small, but mine is even ____________________ .

My favourite chocolate bar is more expensive than it used to be, but it is not the ____________________ expensive chocolate bar in the shop.

Crossing the road by the zebra crossing is less dangerous than crossing by a roundabout, but crossing with the lollipop man is definitely the ____________________ dangerous way to cross.

Choosing adjectives

Adjectives help to make your writing really interesting, but some adjectives work harder than others. Try to avoid using tired adjectives like *nice* or *good*. There are lots of different ways that things can be nice or good. Think of more exciting alternatives instead!

SATs practice

Write these sentences again, replacing the boring adjective with a more interesting alternative.

LEVEL 3 The elephant was big.

____

____

____

LEVEL 4 I am reading an interesting book about dinosaurs.

____

____

____

____

LEVEL 5 My mum was really happy when I won first prize in the writing competition.

____

____

____

____

Homophones

What are homophones?

Homophones are words that sound the same, but are spelt differently. Many of the words we use a lot are homophones, so it is easy to make a mistake by using the wrong one. Most of the time there are just two words to worry about.

which *witch* *hear* *here*

Sometimes there are three or four!

paw pour pore poor

SATs practice

Write down a homophone for each of these words.

 too ______________

LEVEL 4 where ______________

 stares ______________

Choosing the right homophone

Because homophones have different meanings, using the wrong homophone will mean that your writing doesn't make sense.

Read your writing through when you have finished to make sure that you have really said what you think you have!

SATs practice

Underline the correct homophone to complete each sentence.

There were toys and books all over the flaw / floor .

The children put on their / there coats, ready to go home.

The pairs / pears from the tree in our garden taste grate / great .

Spelling rules for suffixes

Simple suffix addition

Suffixes are groups of letters we can add to the ends of some words to alter their meaning.

ly ful ness ing able less free

Most of the time, you can add the suffix without changing the spelling of the root word.

joy + ful = joyful

complete + ly = completely

SATs practice

Match up these words with the correct suffix.

LEVEL 3 — able ful ly

play ______

enjoy ______

sad ______

LEVEL 4 — ly able less

end ______

agree ______

proper ______

LEVEL 5 — ly free able

foresee ______

care ______

sincere ______

Changing *y* to *i*

Sometimes, you need to change the spelling of the root word before you can add a suffix. If the root word ends in a consonant followed by *y*, you have to change the *y* to *i* before you can add a suffix.

happy + er = happier

pretty + ly = prettily

bounty + ful = bountiful

SATs practice

Complete these word sums.

windi + er = ______________________

beauti + ful = ______________________

friendly + er = ______________________

silli + ness = ______________________

reli + able = ______________________

plenty + ful = ______________________

crazy + ly = ______________________

shy + ness = ______________________

silky + ness = ______________________

Synonyms

Looking for new words

Synonyms are words with similar meanings, like *quick* and *fast*. A thesaurus is a special book which lists words with similar meanings, to help you to find new words to use.

SATs practice

Choose a synonym from the box to replace the word in bold type in each sentence.

gobbled	sipped	glowed	grimaced	enough	endless

 The boy **ate** his snack. ______________

 The light bulb **shone** brightly. ______________

LEVEL 5 The chef measured **sufficient** flour to bake the cake. ______________

Adding variety

Synonyms are useful, because they can save you from having to keep using the same words again and again in your writing. This can make your writing more interesting.

SATs practice

Think of a word to replace the bold words in these sentences.

 "Have you done your homework yet?" said James.
"No, not yet," **said** ______________ Max.

 The girls were scared when they heard the noise, because they were **scared** ______________ of the dark.

 Jenny scribbled out what she had written, then **scribbled** ______________ another note.

Choosing synonyms

Very few synonyms have exactly the same meaning, so you need to choose them carefully so that you create exactly the effect that you want to in your writing.

SATs practice

Choose the best synonym to complete the sentences. Circle the one you choose.

The car thumped / hit the lamp-post with a crunch.

The little girl smiled / sneered happily when she opened her birthday present.

The woman organised / arranged the flowers in a vase.

Antonyms

What are antonyms?

Antonyms are words with opposite meanings.

big ⟷ *small*

Not all words have an antonym, but some have more than one.

new ← *old* → *young*

SATs practice

Match up the pairs of antonyms.

LEVEL 3

wide	long
warm	narrow
short	cool

LEVEL 4

leave	full
asleep	arrive
empty	awake

Write down antonyms for these words.

buy ____________________

teacher ____________________

parent ____________________

lost ____________________

Using antonyms

Antonyms help us to describe the difference between things.

*I was **early** for school, but Katie was **late**.*

They can be really useful in our writing. Sometimes an entire story is based on opposites. Think about *Beauty and the Beast!*

SATs practice

Think of antonyms for the words in bold to complete these sentences.

The **huge** elephant was frightened of the ____________ mouse.

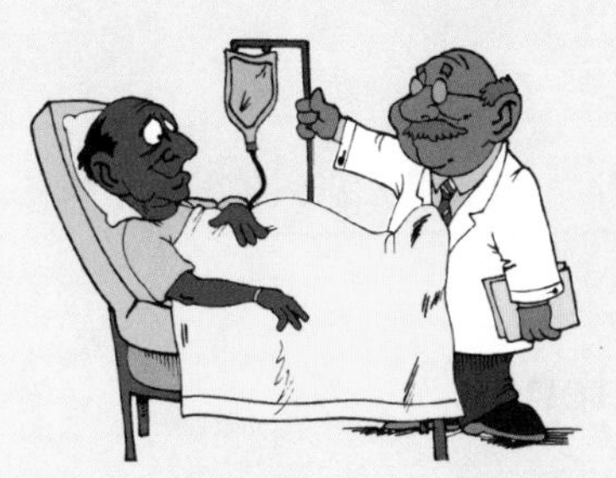

The **doctor** went to see how his ____________ was feeling.

The sun **rose** at 5 am yesterday morning, and ____________ at 8 pm.

How writers create mood

Clever techniques

Creative techniques like onomatopoeia and alliteration can help to paint a picture of what is happening in a story, or create an atmosphere. Even the kind of sentence you use will contribute to the mood. Try using very short sentences to build up suspense!

Experiment with techniques in your own writing and, if you are asked to write about a story, make sure you mention any creative techniques you find.

SATs practice

Imagine that you are trying to create a mysterious, spooky mood for a ghost story you are writing. Think about what the setting might look, sound and smell like, then answer these questions about a secret passageway in the story.

LEVEL 3 Pick the best adjective to describe the passageway.

cramped **spacious** **spotless**

____

LEVEL 4 Choose an onomatopoeia to complete the sentence.

creaked **trickled** **whooshed**

Water ________________ slowly down the mossy walls, forming puddles on the floor.

LEVEL 5 Write a simile to complete this sentence.

The passageway stretched off into the darkness like a

____.

Combining techniques

Good writers use a combination of interesting vocabulary and creative techniques to build up a mood, just like the description of the secret passageway you have just been working on.

Make sure you read a good variety of different stories to give you lots of ideas.

SATs practice

Combine different techniques to complete these sentences about the entrance to a haunted house.

Draw attention to the door of the haunted house in this sentence by using alliteration. You will need to find a synonym to replace one of the adjectives, so that all of the words in the phrase begin with the same sound.

The door was made of shabby, withered wood.

____

____

LEVEL 4 Combine onomatopoeia and an adverb in a sentence.

The old car ***screeched*** *to a halt* ***dramatically***.

Write down your completed sentence.

The heavy old door [onomatopoeia] open [adverb].

____

____

In this sentence, personification has been used to write a metaphor to describe the doorway.

The doorway was a gaping toothless mouth, waiting.

Write another metaphor, using personification, to describe the windows of the deserted house.

____

____

How English is English?

Loanwords

The English language is changing all the time. Throughout history, settlers have brought new words with them and English speakers travelling to other countries have brought words back from other languages. In return, languages all over the world contain words that started out in the English language. Words that are borrowed from another language are called loanwords.

SATs practice

This sentence contains a loanword from the German language. Can you find and underline it?

My friend bought me a glitzy pink top for my birthday.

This sentence contains two loanwords from the French language. Can you find and underline them?

Mum went to the hair salon while the mechanics at the garage fixed the car.

This sentence contains four loanwords from the Italian language. Can you find and underline them?

We had balcony seats at the opera, just above the violin section of the orchestra.

Dialect

The special informal words and phrases used in a particular place are called dialect. The dialects used in different places are often given names. The dialect used in Newcastle is often called 'geordie'. The dialect that originated in the East End of London is often called 'cockney'.

Over time, words from different languages and dialects become part of our everyday language. Every year new words are added to the official Oxford dictionary.

SATs practice

The dialect used in Liverpool is called 'scouse'. Use the rest of this sentence to work out what the red dialect word means. Circle your answer.

I hadn't eaten all day, so I went to find some scran.

food **drink** **sweets**

Read the rest of the sentence to work out what the red scouse words mean. Circle your answers.

I went to the bommie party with my bezzy friend, and we watched the fireworks together.

bommie: **birthday** **bonfire** **Christmas**

bezzy: **oldest** **old** **best**

Read the rest of this sentence to work out what the red scouse words mean.

I borrowed some ackers from my aul'fella to buy some sweets.

ackers ______________________________

aul'fella ______________________________

Instructions

What are instructions?

Instructions are directions on how to do something. Instructions don't ask you what to do – they tell you. There are lots of different types, including recipes, directions on how to build something or signs to get to a particular place. You will also find them on medicines, toiletries and lots of packaged food.

Instructions are written using the imperative, which is how they tell you what to do, rather than asking. The imperative changes the way that the verbs are used. In most ordinary sentences, the word 'to', or a noun or pronoun, comes before the verb.

*You need **to cut** out a circle of card.*

The imperative just uses the verb.

***Cut** out a circle of card.*

SATs practice

Which of these texts is a type of instruction? Circle your answer.

a telephone directory **a recipe** **a story book**

Tick the title that is most likely to belong to a set of instructions.

- Bank Holiday Fun at County Fair ☐
- The Life of Henry VIII ☐
- How to build your chest of drawers ☐

Write this sentence out again, using the imperative verb.

You should not walk on the grass.

____

____

Breaking down the task

Instructions often break tasks down into simple steps. You need to start at the beginning and work your way through, one at a time. Instructions are often numbered to ensure that they are carried out in the correct order.

SATs practice

Put these instructions into the correct order by numbering them.

Squeeze the orange halves to extract the juice. ☐

Buy five fresh oranges. ☐

Ask an adult to slice each orange in half. ☐

Chill the juice before drinking. ☐

Read the set of instructions below, then think of a suitable title for them.

____

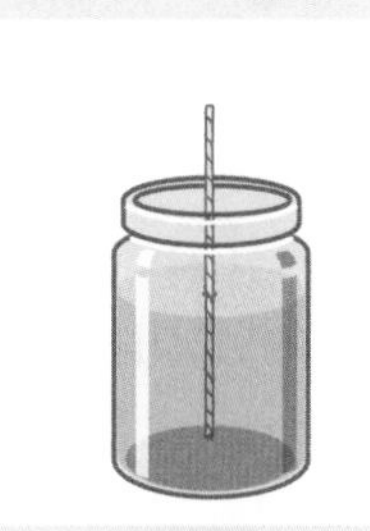

1 Add a tablespoon of salt to a jar of warm water.

2 ____

____

3 When the salt has dissolved, hang a length of string over the edge of the jar, so that the end is in the salt solution.

4 Leave your jar in a safe place for several days and check regularly for signs of salt crystals on the string.

Step 2 is missing from the instructions above. Using the picture to help you, write in a sensible sentence for step 2. Don't forget to use the imperative.

Persuasive writing

Types of persuasive writing

Persuasive writing is writing that is designed to make the reader adopt a particular viewpoint, or want to buy a product or visit a particular attraction. Adverts in newspapers and magazines, and on the Internet, are examples of persuasive writing. So are many leaflets and posters.

SATs practice

In which of the following would you **not** expect to see persuasive writing? Tick the **two** correct boxes.

on a poster publicising a show ☐ in a fairy tale ☐ on a road sign ☐

Which of these two things is an example of persuasive writing? Underline your answer.

a postcard of a castle, from the gift shop

a leaflet about a castle, from the tourist information centre

Give three examples of persuasive writing that are not already mentioned in the questions on this page.

____________ ____________ ____________

Choosing language

Most good persuasive writing does not include many words, so every word you use has to count. Think about your audience. You will probably choose different words if you are aiming your writing at children, for example.

SATs practice

Read this sentence, then answer the questions.

The UK's tallest roller coaster, the eagerly-awaited Vortex, will thrill its first lucky passengers this weekend!

LEVEL 3 Find and copy **two** persuasive words from the sentence.

LEVEL 4 Which adjective has the writer used to describe the roller coaster?

LEVEL 5 Write the sentence again, using persuasive writing ideas of your own.

Setting out your writing

Persuasive writing is not always set out in complete sentences. You can make use of limited space by using bullet points, sub-headings and text boxes. You can also underline key words, or put them in a different colour. Think carefully about the title of your writing to make it really catchy.

SATs practice

Opening SOON!

Slalom, the region's newest and biggest dry ski slope, is opening soon!

Slalom offers the very latest dry slope technology, plus a lively bar and restaurant for après-ski fun.

- 300m ski slope
- 3 nursery slopes
- ski lift on main slope

SPECIAL OCCASIONS

Slalom can cater for weddings, kids' parties and corporate functions.

LEVEL 3 Underline a sub-heading in this piece of advertising.

LEVEL 4 Underline **two** key words in the first sentence that you think should stand out.

LEVEL 5 Think of a title for the bullet points.

Reports

What are reports?

Reports are pieces of factual writing about a particular topic. Because they can be on anything from insects to Vikings, you will probably find that you write reports in lots of different classes, not just English.

Reports are organised into topics. They do not need to be written in chronological order and they are often written in the present tense.

Ladybirds are familiar visitors to many gardens and they eat the aphids that do so much damage to plants.

SATs practice

Decide whether you think these statements about reports are true or false.

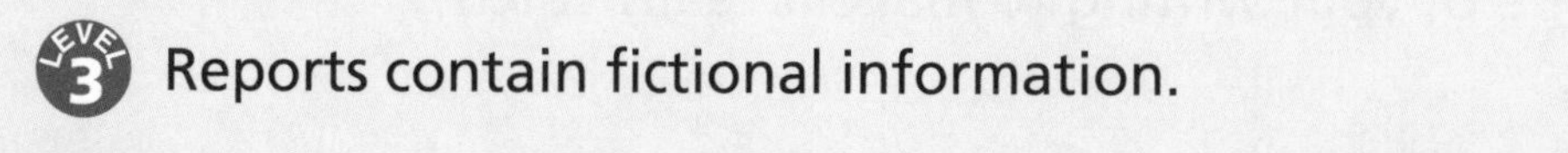

LEVEL 3 Reports contain fictional information. ________

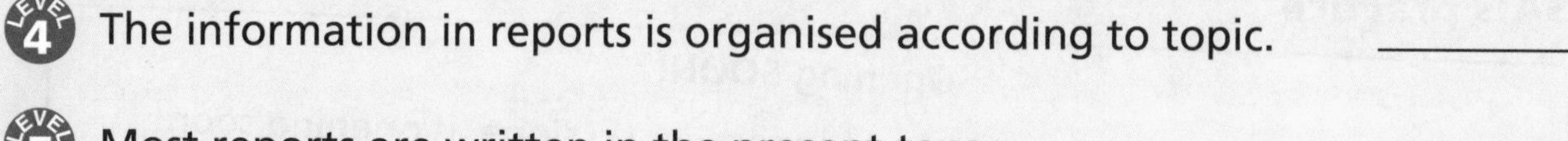

LEVEL 4 The information in reports is organised according to topic. ________

LEVEL 5 Most reports are written in the present tense. ________

Planning reports

It can be difficult to organise your information into topics for a report, but once you have a structure you can simply write a paragraph for each topic area. Start by researching your topic in books and on the Internet. Decide which information you want to use, then try using a spidergram to help you to organise similar ideas into separate topic areas.

Spidergrams help you to organise your ideas and you should make sure you don't leave out anything important when you come to write the report.

You can also try using tree diagrams, flow charts or notes on sticky paper.

SATs practice

Circle the ideas on this spidergram using different colours to match the key.

Green = plants and trees, Red = animals and birds, Blue = mini-beasts

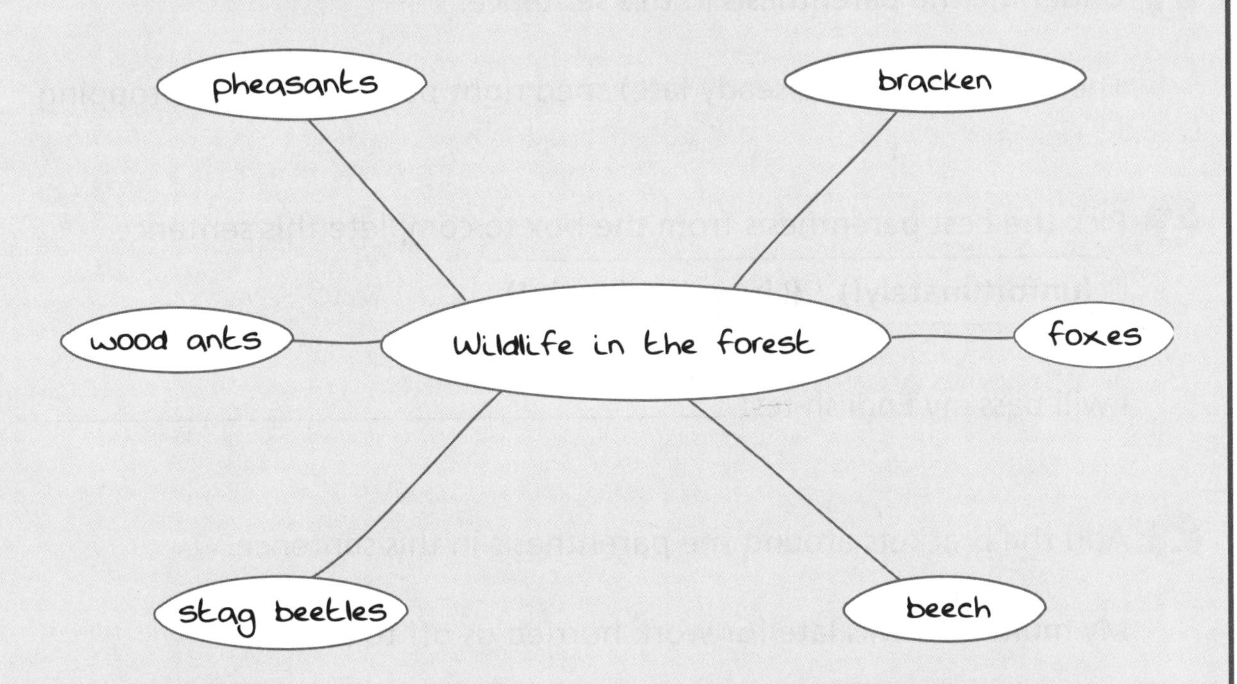

Add these extra topics to the spidergram, following the colour key.

badgers nettles spiders

Think of one more idea for each topic area, then add them to the spidergram, following the colour key.

Adding information

Parenthesis

Parenthesis is one way of giving your reader more information about what they are reading. It means adding words to sentences, in brackets.

Parenthesis can work in different ways. Sometimes, it is an explanation of something.

The dog (who was soaking wet from the rain) shook himself all over me.

Parenthesis can also add an afterthought to a sentence.

The dog shook himself all over me (again!).

SATs practice

Underline the parenthesis in this sentence.

The bus (which was already late) sped right past us, without stopping.

Pick the best parenthesis from the box to complete this sentence.

(unfortunately!) (I hope!) (again!)

I will pass my English test ______________________________.

Add the brackets around the parenthesis in this sentence.

My mum who was late for work hurried us off to school.

Footnotes

Footnotes are another way of adding extra information. They are found at the bottom, or foot, of the page, and are used to give extra information about the writing on the page.

They sometimes explain the meaning of difficult words too, instead of a glossary. Both fiction and non-fiction books can have footnotes.

SATs practice

LEVEL 3 Is this sentence about footnotes true or false? ____________________

Footnotes are found at the back of a book.

LEVEL 4 Where else in a book might you be able to find the meaning of a difficult word?

____

LEVEL 5 Write down **two** jobs that footnotes do.

____

____

____

____

____

Recounts

Features of recounts

Recounts tell readers about something that has happened. The events are described in the order in which they happened, using the past tense.

An account of a school trip, a story about something funny that happened to you, or a piece of biographical writing would all be classed as recounts.

Timelines or flow charts help you to put events into the correct order. Then, when you write your report, your timeline will ensure nothing gets left out.

SATs practice

Look at these pictures, which are in the wrong order.

☐ ☐ ☐ ☐

Write a sentence to describe what is happening in the first picture.

___

Number the pictures, to put the recount into the correct order.

Write a sentence for each picture in the correct order and in the past tense, to complete the recount.

___

___

___

___

Using time connectives

The different events in a recount are often joined together using time connectives like *when, afterwards, some time later* and *in the end*. These connectives help to make the writing flow better and ensure that the reader understands the order in which the various events took place.

SATs practice

Underline the time connectives in this recount.

We found a stray cat in our garden. Mum rang the local animal rescue centre and afterwards we put up posters around the town. After that we waited for her owners to get in touch. Eventually we realised that nobody was going to claim her, so in the end we decided to adopt her.

Join up the pairs of time connectives with similar meanings.

first	all at once
then	finally
in the end	to begin with
suddenly	next

Add the missing time connectives to this recount.

After when then Next Later

I was on my way to school ________ I saw a wallet lying in the gutter. ________ I had made sure its owner wasn't nearby, I took the wallet to the police station. ________ , I had to fill in a form and ________ a policeman drove me to school in a police car. ________ that day the police rang to say that a man had collected his wallet and left a reward for me.

Characters

What is a character?

Characters are the personalities that take part in a story. Characters are usually people, but they can also be animals, toys or anything that you can imagine having a story about!

They are the most important part of any story, because, if they seem real, people are much more likely to want to find out what happens to them.

SATs practice

Read this extract from a story and answer the questions.

A dark shadow fell across the opening and the pair pressed their bodies back into the shadows, terrified of being seen. The shadow slinked slowly by and Violet relaxed a little. Danny flopped onto the floor and tried to stifle a rumble from his stomach. "I'm starving!" he whispered. "Do you think it's safe to go out now?"

"How should I know?" hissed back Violet. She didn't mean to be cross with him, but sometimes she resented having to take charge all the time. It wasn't as if she was older, after all.

Always the braver of the two, Violet finally edged silently to the mouth of the hole, then scuttled along the skirting board in the direction of the fridge. If Danny didn't eat soon, she reasoned, his rumbling tummy would give them both away.

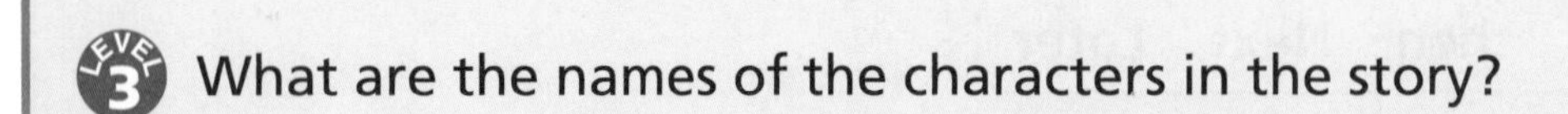

LEVEL 3 What are the names of the characters in the story?

____

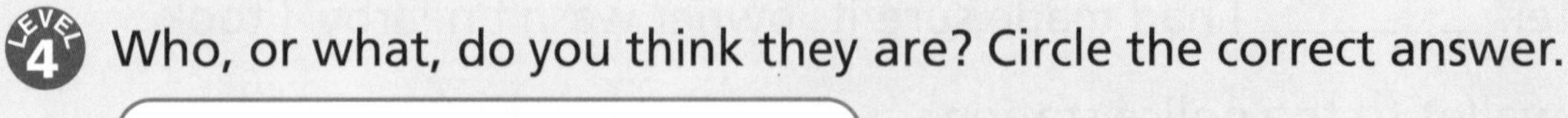

LEVEL 4 Who, or what, do you think they are? Circle the correct answer.

spiders **children** **mice**

LEVEL 5 One of the characters will go on a dangerous journey later in the story. Based on what you have read so far, which one do you think it will be?

____

Developing characters

Good characters need to be developed carefully, so they seem real. Think about the role they are going to play in the story and try to give them characteristics that fit with what you want them to do in the story.

What your characters look like is only part of their profile. Imagine how they would think or feel if they were real people. Then use words that build up the picture. So a shy little girl might *giggle nervously* or *shuffle awkwardly*.

You could try basing a character on someone you know, or even yourself, to make it easier to imagine how they might think, feel and behave.

SATs practice

Here are some familiar characters from the fairy tale Little Red Riding Hood. You probably know more about them than you think, because of the way their characters are developed in the story.

LEVEL 3 All three characters went to bed last night. Which one sipped a warming cup of cocoa, then pulled on a snug night-cap and woolly bed socks?

___

LEVEL 4 Which character would be most likely to tell a lie?

___

LEVEL 5 Which character would be the most likely to notice that someone looked different from normal?

___

Openings and endings

Story starters

The first lines of a story are very important. They draw the reader in and make them want to read more. Good story openings leave a question unanswered, so the readers want to read on to find out what happens.

Good story starters use lots of descriptive language too, to bring the action to life.

SATs practice

Read this story opening, then answer the questions about it.

Olivia was surprised to find nobody there when she answered the ringing doorbell. Instead, quivering and whining mysteriously on the doorstep, was a brown box, pierced with air-holes and marked, quite clearly, with her name.

Dad came up the hallway, smiling mischievously. "Go on, birthday girl, have a look inside," he said.

LEVEL 3 What is the question left unanswered in this story opening?

Why was there nobody at the door? ☐

What is in the box? ☐

Why is Dad smiling? ☐

Olivia

LEVEL 4 What do you think is inside the parcel? Then write down **two** words or phrases that give you a clue.

_______________ _______________ _______________

LEVEL 5 Some writers start their stories with one of the characters speaking. Rewrite the opening sentence, starting with Dad's speech.

____

____

Ending your story

Story endings are important too. If your story just trails off into nothing, your readers will be disappointed. They might not even realise that the story has finished!

Good endings give your reader something to think about after they have finished the story. Perhaps the characters are left in a dangerous situation, a nasty character is punished or everything works out for the best.

Some stories have a twist in the tale, where something completely unexpected happens right at the end. Others have a moral lesson in their ending, like a fable.

Whatever ending you choose, you must have it planned all the way through, so it doesn't seem 'tacked on' to the end.

SATs practice

You have just been working on the opening for a story. Read what happens in the middle and then think about a good ending.

> ## *The story so far…*
>
> *Olivia has been given a puppy for her birthday. The boy next door is jealous and starts saying unkind things about Olivia at school, but she ignores him. This makes him even more angry, so one cold wet night he creeps out of his house and lets the dog out and it runs away.*

LEVEL 3 If the story had a happy ending, what might happen?

____

LEVEL 4 The writer of the story wants to punish the boy who let the dog out. How could the ending include that?

____

____

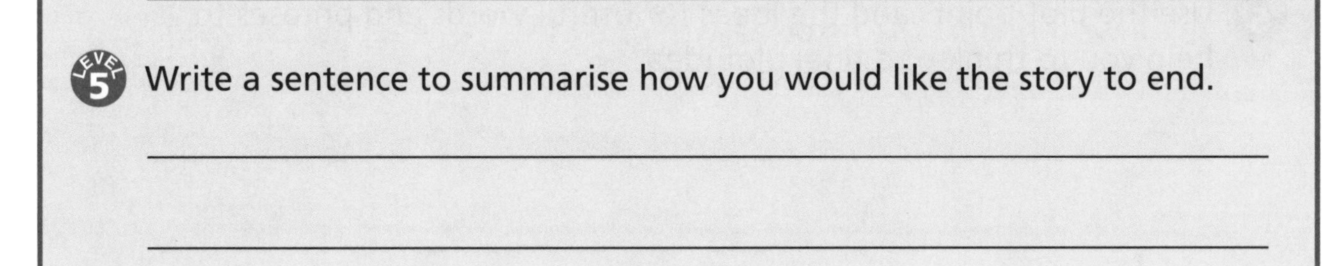

LEVEL 5 Write a sentence to summarise how you would like the story to end.

____

____

Plotting

Clustering ideas

You will probably have lots of ideas for your story before you start writing it. Clustering is a good way to organise your ideas before you start to plan the story in detail.

Think of a word that describes the main idea for your story, then let your mind wander and make a note of any useful words or phrases that you could use in the story, as well as ideas for how the story could develop. Draw lines or arrows between ideas that are connected.

SATs practice

Have a look at this clustering, then answer the questions.

Pirates

Useful words: creaking rigging, figurehead, skull and crossbones

Creative phrases: ship slipped silently through the sea; sand as fine as icing sugar

befriends son of the librarian and takes him to the beach to see the ship

girl on holiday finds trap door leading to secret beach and sees an old pirate ship

finds book in library and realises the pirate attack really did take place, but 200 years before

overhears pirates plotting to take over village – nobody believes her

Can you think of some more useful words to describe the pirate ship?

____

Use arrows to link up the different plot ideas in a sensible order.

Use the plot points and the ideas for useful words and phrases to help you to think of a final plot idea.

____

____

Stages in a story plan

Stories are like a sandwich. The beginning and the ending are the slices of bread, with most of the action in between, like a filling. This filling usually presents the characters with a problem to overcome and follows their progress until the problem is resolved in the ending.

The more you practise planning, the easier you will find it.

SATs practice

Read this story plan, then answer the questions.

Opening: introduces the characters and setting.

Build-up: allows the events running up to the big dilemma to unfold.

The children are bored because it is raining, so they start to throw a ball about in the house. The ball knocks over a vase and breaks it.

The dilemma: explains the problem the characters have to overcome.

Should the children own up or try to put it right themselves?

The events: tells how the characters try to overcome the problem.

The children see if they can find a replacement in a local shop.

The resolution: tells how the characters resolve the problem posed in the story.

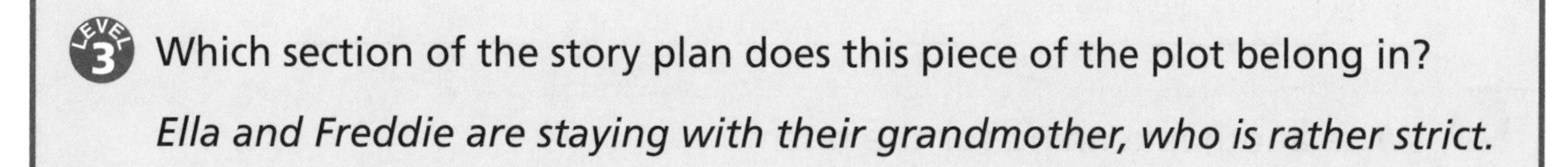

LEVEL 3 Which section of the story plan does this piece of the plot belong in?

Ella and Freddie are staying with their grandmother, who is rather strict.

____

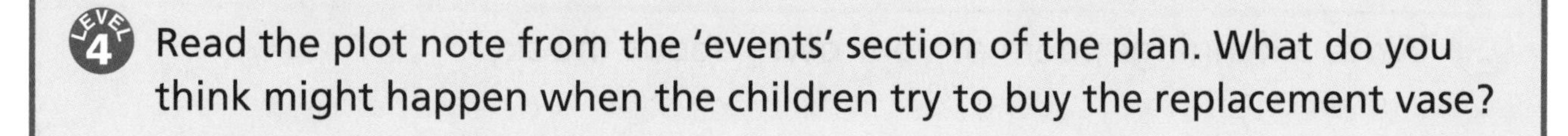

LEVEL 4 Read the plot note from the 'events' section of the plan. What do you think might happen when the children try to buy the replacement vase?

____

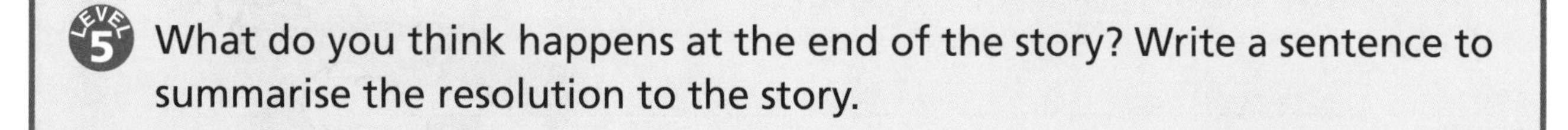

LEVEL 5 What do you think happens at the end of the story? Write a sentence to summarise the resolution to the story.

____

Poetry

Kennings

Writing poetry can be a bit scary, but there are simple poetry styles that give you the perfect opportunity to show just how creatively you can use language!

Kennings are a type of poem. They describe something without actually saying what the thing is. They have been used for centuries, particularly in old English and Norse poetry.

SATs practice

Read this kennings poem then answer the questions.

Beach-washer

Boat-rocker

Wreck-maker

Treasure-keeper

LEVEL 3 What do you think the poem is about?

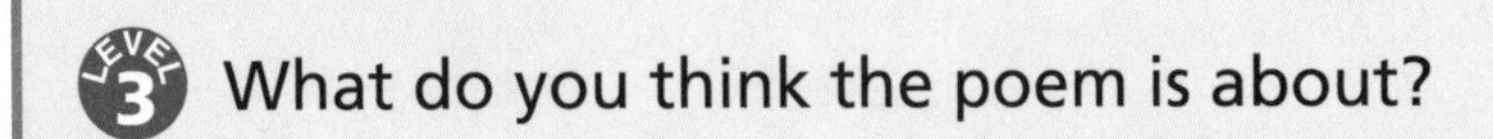

LEVEL 4 Write another kenning for the poem.

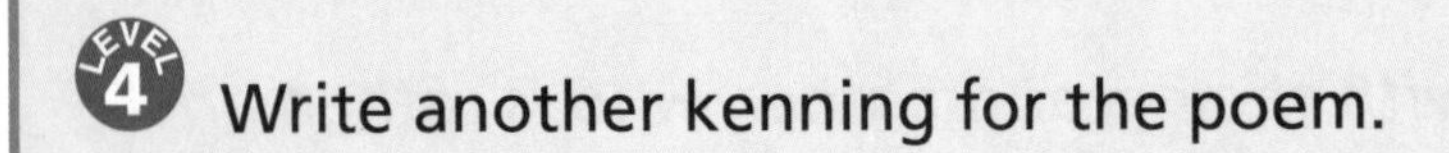

LEVEL 5 Write a kennings poem of your own, about the sky.

List poems

List poems are another simple way to write fabulous poetry. They are simply lists of descriptions but, unlike kennings poems, they often say what they are describing, right at the top.

Cold is . . .
the first winds of winter,
soft snow fall
ice cubes in fruit juice,
frost on a window pane.

SATs practice

Now read this list poem, then answer the questions.

Summer is . . .
golden sunshine,
light evenings,
eating outdoors,
beach days,

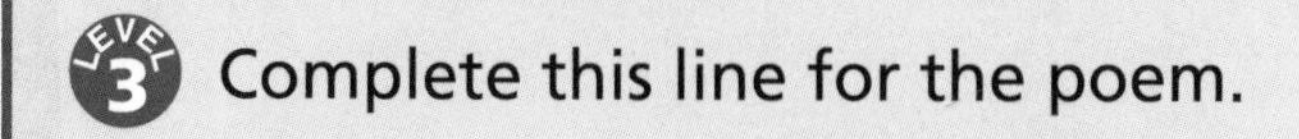

LEVEL 3 Complete this line for the poem.

The smell of ______________________________.

LEVEL 4 Add another line of your own to the list poem.

LEVEL 5 Write a similar list poem about the winter.

Notes

Your notes